# THE PRAYER
# CONNECTION

## A True Story of
## Miracles

**Gloria and Robert Mascarelli**

**The Prayer Connection**
Copyright © 2000 by Gloria and Robert Mascarelli

Published by Miracle Book Publishers
Printed in the United States of America

Cover design and graphics by George Gallo

Mr. Robert Mascarelli
C/O Miracle Book Publishers
PO Box 429
Patchogue, NY 11772     Fax: (516) 207-3175

Unless otherwise noted, Scripture references are taken from the *New American Standard Bible*, the *Open Bible Edition,* copyright 1960, 1962, 1963, 1968, 1971, 1972, 1973, 1975, 1977. Used by permission.
"A Nicotine Lollipop to Help Smokers Quit." Copyright © 1991 by the New York Times Co. Reprinted by permission.

The authors and Publisher of this book state that the views expressed in its content reflect the subjective experiences of the authors and that the book's intended purpose is for inspirational reading only. The book is not intended to serve as a model for prayer.

### Publishers Cataloging-in-Publication

Mascarelli, Gloria.
    The prayer connection : a true story of
miracles / Gloria and Robert Mascarelli. -- 1st ed.
    p. cm.
    LCCN: 99-74732
    ISBN: 0-9643376-0-7

    1. Mascarelli, Robert. 2. Mascarelli, Gloria.
3. Christian biography--New York (State)--
Patchogue. 4. Prayer. 5. Miracles. 6. Angels.
I. Mascarelli, Robert. II. Title.

BR1700.2.M37 1999
277.47/25/08290922          QB199-1081

Ordering instructions:
See back of book for information about ordering additional copies.
For large volume and organizational discounts please contact the Publisher at the address listed above or call toll free 1 (800) 478-7188

This book is dedicated to Almighty God in accordance with the specific promise made in Bob's journal entry dated "late April, 1990."

# Acknowledgments

We are fortunate to have a talented family whose contributions to this book have been invaluable. We appreciate all their help. Valerie Spielman, Bob's daughter wisely choose our title, *The Prayer Connection*. Gloria's two daughters, Cynthia Gallo and Cheryl Khalou made suggestions that directed us to fill in important details which would have otherwise been omitted. George Gallo, our son-in-law cheerfully gave his time to design and execute our cover art. Raymond Mascarelli, Bob's brother, deserves many thanks from both of us for supporting our efforts to get published. His wife Carol contributed her editing skills.

We would also like to thank the following people: Professor Jill Furst for her editorial corrections and encouraging comments, Rose George of Bradley Publications for her help with marketing ideas and Ann Tower of National Religious Broadcasters for her patience while answering our many inquiries. We thank you all for your informative chats and cheerful responses to our questions

Dr. John Harford and his wife Dr. Esther Chang, two Christians of great faith, welcomed us into their home and took valuable time from their busy schedules to read our manuscript. We thank you for your encouragement.

Bob's special thanks go to John Germuga and Don Martin, two of the leaders of the Tres Dias weekend who, with good humor, welcomed a skeptic in their midst.

VI

# Preface

I began writing a personal diary in April of 1990. The activity of recording my thoughts and experiences continued for three and a half years.

The journal was motivated by my desire to keep a record of my attempts to break through my agnosticism to reach a God I thought of as either unreal or inaccessible. Because of my doubts and my unfamiliarity with prayer, I approached God with many requests and challenges. These communications were chronicled in my diary entries. I imagine that I tested God's patience with all my demands. If there are jobs allotted in Heaven, I'll probably be found with a potato peeler in hand.

I soon learned that God not only existed, but that He was readily willing to interact with me personally. Because I was a skeptic, I asked for concrete evidence of His presence, and He responded by offering proof through miraculous events. My journal documents the growth of my faith through revelations, angelic interventions and signs and wonders.

Why did God ask me to keep my diary and faith a secret for over three years?

I believe that a loving God who reaches out to mankind touches the heart of each seeker differently. During His earthly ministry, Jesus reached out to each individual in unique ways according to their individual needs. Some were healed by touch; others by command and others simply because they had faith. God healed me of my unbelief in ways that were appropriate to my personality. God knew me better than I knew myself. He knew my stubbornness, my skepticism and my need for some tangible evidence of His existence. He knew that if I shared my experiences with others, especially my wife, that their interpretations would disrupt my own conclusions. He also knew that I feared being branded as a religious fanatic which was an assessment that was in direct contrast with my self-image at that time. Parting with my "macho" facade was a difficult struggle for me.

God knew I needed to experience my relationship with Him over a period of time before I would be ready to proclaim Him Lord of my life without any doubts or reservations. He commanded my silence, thereby isolating me from the assessment of others, while He presented me with the wondrous miracles through which I can now boldly witness to others. For me to become a soldier of God I needed lots of ammunition and He gave me more than enough. The three and a half years I spent in isolated conversation with God was truly my "Higher" education. I needed that amount of time to earn my degree in faith before I had the confidence to call myself a Christian.

Many times God gave me confirmation of His will through my wife's parallel experiences. Those events revealed the activity and counsel of the Holy Spirit in both our lives. The revelations and miraculous signs that were presented to both of us and others we know, leave no doubt in my mind that God had preordained the events to occur just as they happened.

All praise be to Jesus who has answered my prayers in wondrous ways. He has given me this book as a vehicle to glorify Him.

Robert Mascarelli
July 1999

# Contents

# The Prayer Connection

# Chapter 1

## The Journey Begins

This is a true story about a man who kept a secret. That man is my husband, Robert Patrick Mascarelli.

For three and a half years, he furtively kept a personal journal in which he revealed his intimate thoughts. Its focus was to track his skeptical and hesitant steps towards reaching an Almighty God whose existence he doubted. Although the first entry was dated April, 1990, I did not discover its existence until we arrived in Israel in the Fall of 1993.

Prior to leaving on the trip, I was told to expect a surprise, the unveiling of a new project, which would not be shared with me until we arrived on our planned vacation. Immediately after checking into our hotel, Bob informed me that he was going for a long walk and told me that I was to read what he'd left for me on the desk. He provided me with a voice activated tape recorder so that I could record my comments, if any, during the reading of his journal. The word "amazing" and the phrase "I can't believe you kept this a secret from me," were my most frequent and significant comments during the hours that it took me to finish reading the diary

The journal revealed over three years of Bob's secret experiments with prayer. Since our marriage, ten years prior to the first journal entry, I'd regarded Bob as an unbelieving skeptic, a characterization that he readily acknowledged was well-suited at that time. His journal revealed quite a different person, one with whom I was hardly familiar. Bob had a secret self, one that he would share only with the God he wasn't quite sure existed. I was not enlightened about his growing faith during the entire time he recorded his diary entries. Bob had proscribed certain conditions that would have to be met by the Lord before he'd be willing to share any of his secret life with me or anyone else.

At the close of the journal, Bob wrote a note requesting me to begin a plan for my new project. He asked me to organize and assemble his written entries into a readable book. I have always been his voice at the typewriter. We'd worked together in literary efforts before, contributing to and authoring books about Oriental antiques.

At the start of this project, we decided that it would be crucial that I state my own opinions and commentary regarding some of the extraordinary happenings in our lives both prior to and during the time of the writing of the diary. My personal retrospective comments are identified within the quoted text of Bob's diary entries whenever it is necessary to add clarity to his story or to show the dramatic intervention of God's will in our lives through both our perspectives.

When Bob began to record his journal he was not a believer in God, the Bible, miracles or angelic interventions. He was a self-deterministic skeptic who had suddenly found a crying need for a God that he had ignored all his life. He sought to challenge God to deliver him from his situation and to prove that He was real. Moreover, he arrogantly sought proof many times, frequently asking God to perform miracles for him.

God not only proved Himself to Bob by answering his prayers one by one (no matter how unreasonable), He also performed signs and wonders, enacted solely for our edification and need at a time of great personal sorrow. God captured Bob's attention in concrete ways that could not be assigned to chance, luck or coincidence. His answers affected our lives with changes I never would have anticipated and were not always what we would have wished. God did provide us with reasons for each answer in due time, however.

Throughout the years of his journal accounts, many of God's miracles passed right by me without my recognition. They were tailor made by the Lord to catch the personal attention of my husband, and to add credence to his growing faith. The Lord ministered to him through both the joyful and tragic events that are revealed in his journal entries.

We wish to inform the reader that although this is an autobiographical book about religious experiences, it is not a book about denominational religion. Bob has become, however, a confirmed believer in the Trinity of God and the power of prayer as a means of direct communication with Him. Bob can no longer question

His existence and the reality of an eternal life after experiencing what He did first hand.

My personal reliance in God was established before Bob's adventure with the Lord took place, but I was not growing in my Christian life. I was, in fact, a recurrent backslider, not steadily welcoming the Holy Spirit to lead me into a deeper knowledge of God's plan for me. Years ago, a minister prophesied saying, "You will not allow sin in your home. You will have a great unshakable faith. You will be an overcomer." I had no idea, at that time, of the path I was going to travel to realize these prophesies.

Then God involved me in Bob's miracles.

My husband's personal friends and other close family members have long known him as a fun-loving individual, but they also know that he is rather guarded about revealing his private emotions. He has rarely confessed any deep personal need to anyone, not even to me. This written account, exposing his intimate diary entries, reveals many personal thoughts that he ordinarily would not want to publicize. He has opted to do so now because it is the way he's chosen to glorify the God who has given him such a monumental faith and concrete assurance of eternal life. Bob's diary and my comments tell it all.

Although I have been granted poetic license to paraphrase his words, as well as omit some repetitive entries, Bob attests to the fact that the events portrayed are faithful to the accounts in his diary. The story that you are about to read is candidly honest and totally true.

Unless you are already a believer, or would like to be one, please consider carefully if you want to read on.

Accepting what has happened in our lives as true requires some suspension of preconceived notions of what seem to be natural occurrences in nature. Your mind may be preset to disbelieve that some of the described events are really supernatural, and we don't want to encourage anyone to scoff at the miraculous works of God. If you are a skeptic, as Bob was not too long ago, but have enough curiosity to decide to read the book anyway, be prepared to be challenged by what you read.

You will not see the Lord portrayed as a distant Heavenly Father. You will see Him as we have learned Him to be, an active participant in human lives and an intimate friend. Furthermore, you will learn that He is still in the habit of performing amazing miracles, some to answer direct prayer, some to instruct and some to give revelation. You will also learn that God may use ordinary people to serve as His angels or may have angels appear as ordinary people. If you trust what we have written, you will have no choice but to acknowledge the existence of God. You may even find yourself wanting to seek out a personal relationship with Him too.

You will see through our experiences that faith in God does not always shield us from the heartache and evil that exists in this world, but it certainly does provide insulation against irreparable hurt. Faith is capable of turning tragic events into personal victories that are life changing. You will read about how God turned Bob's life upside down and delivered him from disappointment and anguish to peace and joy.

Read on to learn of how a skeptic's prayers were heard and answered by God. Bob's life, as it is recorded in his journal, is a living testimony to the bibical truth,

> "Ask, and it shall be given to you; seek and you shall find; knock, and it shall be opened to you." (Matthew 7:7)

# Chapter 2

## My Brother, My Keeper

In June of 1989, my brother Raymond invited me to attend a nondenominational religious retreat called a Tres Dias Weekend. Without hesitating, I immediately refused.

I'd always considered myself a skeptic as far as the supernatural, parapsychology, fortune telling, astrology and other superstitious matters are concerned. I tended to place God in the same category, although I'd never completely discounted the possibility of a Supreme Creator. I certainly didn't feel that I was searching for God at the time of Raymond's invitation. My notions of God were agnostic and filled with confusion, but I felt no particular yearning to discover the "truth." I'd been a freethinker all my adult life.

Although I was well aware that evil exists in the world, I didn't attribute its existence to a supernatural force or Satanic origin. I did acknowledge that Jesus was a real person and as such, was the most believable part of the trinity. I understood the Bible to be a book that had moral relevance and was historically substantiated to a great degree by recent archaeological discoveries but, I never acknowledged it as the true word of God. Reading the Bible as a book confused me, and frankly, I never felt the need to make a serious attempt at all. If God really was my creator, I had enough arrogance to think He had done a pretty good job. I have always had a strong moral sense of right and wrong. I was sure that my conscience kept me pretty well within the scope of the golden rule of doing unto others as I would have them do unto me. I felt fully responsible for my decisions and regarded my fate as a direct consequence of my personal choices.

My wife Gloria had quite a different idea about God. Raised in a Jewish environment, she always believed in God's covenant with Abraham and the eventuality of a coming Messiah. By accepting the Torah (the first five books of the Old Testament) as her heritage, she acknowledged the Bible as the true word of God. Shortly after we met, she was befriended by someone who declared herself to be a "Jew for Jesus." After a period of introspection and a thorough reading of the New Testament, Gloria accepted "Y'shua" (the Hebrew name of Jesus), as the true Messiah.

My marriage to Gloria created an odd tangle of religious beliefs in our joint family. I was a non-practicing Catholic, and Gloria was a somewhat committed non-practicing "Hebrew Christian." My children, who were all baptized as Catholic, were now attending a Lutheran Church, since my former wife adopted the religion of her new husband. Gloria's children were Jewish, attending their high holy day services with their father. This lack of cohesive religious orientation in my household did not concern me one bit, however. As a matter of fact, it did not bother me at all. God simply was not one of my concerns, and I certainly didn't think He'd be at all concerned with me.

Raymond had asked me to attend the Tres Dias weekend many times before. My refusal to go was anticipated. This time he'd devised a strategy to force me to agree. He began by telling me that Gloria wanted to participate in the women's weekend, but that I was required to attend two weeks before her. According to him, by refusing to go, I was holding her back from something that was important to her. This argument wasn't enough to convince me.

Then he hit me with the ultimate of "guilt trips." He reminded me of the last time he cared for my mentally ill daughter after her release from the hospital. He personally ministered to Regina's needs night and day, sacrificing his family life for her welfare. He also recounted an earlier occasion when she escaped from the hospital and he sheltered her until she was willing to return. Ray insisted that his devotion to my daughter was a reflection of his love for me. He was now asking me to return this love by agreeing to attend the retreat.

"You owe me this," he said with a smile. He knew he had me. His phrasing left no room for me to finagle out of the situation. I knew that any negative answer I could give, even if I could find a plausible one, would be interpreted as a personal insult to him. He had me over a barrel. I owed him a favor, and he wouldn't take no for an answer. I had no choice but to say yes.

I had no idea why he considered me a candidate for the weekend, since Tres Dias is designed for committed Christians as a rekindling of their faith. I knew this and I was very apprehensive about going. I felt completely outside the world of religion. I forced myself to think of the weekend as a good deed that I was performing for Raymond and Gloria. A good deed I could do, but I wasn't going to like it.

The worst part was going to revolve around the issue of smoking. I was told that the only place I could smoke was in the men's room. I was accustomed to inhaling over three packs a day and I couldn't conceive of going too long without a cigarette. As a matter of fact, I did spend as much time as possible in the men's room. By the end of the weekend, the guys teased me about my compulsive bathroom habits.

When I wasn't busy puffing away, I was frankly surprised to hear the sincere testimonies of Christian men, men like me who I considered regular guys. They came from different backgrounds and occupations and seemed normal enough to suit me. Yet, they spoke about a God whom I didn't know, and they spoke with a passion and emotion that was foreign to my experience, making me feel even more like an outsider than I had before I arrived.

My brother attended the weekend as a singing musician. It's long been a family joke that he can't sing on key. To accompany himself, he played the guitar, another source of family ridicule. The fact that he admittedly and obviously did neither very well, didn't seem to matter to him. He said he was singing to praise God.

That was fine with me, as long as his voice and playing were drowned out by other people.

I'd gradually learned to accept Ray's religiousness since it suddenly emerged about seven years ago. At first I was threatened by the changes I saw in my restless, pleasure-seeking brother. I was comfortable with him just the way he was, and I didn't want him to change at all. The "born again" Raymond had even less appeal to our father, who never attends church. He considers himself to be a good Catholic nevertheless, because he says he's too old to sin anymore.

I'd originally hoped that Ray's churchiness would phase out over the years and that religion would turn out to be just another of his passing interests, like his last enthusiastic fling with astronomy. There had been a long list of diversions before that. I figured he'd go on to another hobby when he tired of this God business. When he started a Bible class at his house, I knew he was serious. When he gave up his weekly card game, I knew the change was permanent. I decided that religion was his business as long as he didn't bother me too much about it. Anyway, these were the reasons why I ended up going to a religious retreat at which I felt completely out of place.

The fact that I was baptized and confirmed as a child, and that I had occasionally prayed didn't mean that I was a Christian in the way those other men were. They all knew the Bible and believed every word. They were committed to God and I was a big question mark. I had a casual knowledge of Bible stories as presented in the movies and on television, but anytime I'd picked up a Bible I'd been discouraged by the confusing language.

Moreover, the idea that there really was a Moses who didn't look like Charlton Heston was inconceivable to me. I didn't even try to hide my ignorance at the retreat. Everyone knew I was there only because I couldn't refuse my brother. We all had a good laugh when I innocently left the room and the door was blocked by two of the men who thought I was attempting an escape. I was warmly accepted at face value, and, surprisingly, I enjoyed myself.

The weekend gave me a lot to think about. It was as good a time as any to experiment with prayer since I was surrounded by it. As a matter of fact, I would have felt more embarrassed by not attempting to pray than I would by faking it. The environment of the retreat made it almost feel natural. It was the first time I ever stood alongside other men in prayer. I definitely felt awkward at the beginning, but their sincerity was contagious. I suppose it was my first real adult effort to make contact with a God whom I'd thought of as a stranger, if he was indeed there at all. The men around me were immersed in their faith. Their obvious belief in God stimulated my curiosity and it made it possible for me to experiment. I was frankly amazed at their commitment.

I was impressed by the personal testimonies that I heard. Most of the men described their coming to Christ as a kind of rescue. One after another, they revealed themselves as people who had experienced great difficulties such as physical ailments, emotional problems, deep grief, burdens of sin or shame. They claimed that Jesus had brought them out of their discomforts into a new life. I finally got a glimpse of what Ray's being "born again" is about. I knew however, I was far from feeling that their need for salvation applied to me.

I had trouble thinking of myself as a sinner, although I was aware that I had done things in the past that I am deeply ashamed of now. I had a problem with the whole concept of sin. As a child I was taught that some sins were worse than others and needed lengthy penance. This has made it very easy for me to rationalize most of my bad behavior as being relatively unimportant. From hearing the testimonies at the weekend, I began to understand that from a bibical perspective, all sin has accountability, even if we succeed in rationalizing it away. Furthermore, I learned that if a person confesses his sins, his petition for forgiveness should be made directly to Jesus.

The practice of confessing sins on a one to one basis with an invisible God made the act of confession much more palatable to me. The necessity of physically entering a confessional booth to relate my sins, one of the requirements of my childhood Catholic upbringing, discouraged me from going to church. I was just too embarrassed to tell the priest.

I also remembered my adult reaction to the change in the Church's policy regarding eating meat on Friday. I grew up believing that any violation of this dietary law was a sin against God. Later, I learned that the law prohibiting the ingestion of meat on Friday is not even in the Bible. It was just a Catholic tradition that has since been changed. All those pizzas that I was forced to eat when I really wanted a hamburger instead, all those "white lies" I told my mother about forgetting that it was Friday when she asked what I had for lunch, all the guilt I felt was proved unnecessary by the changes made in church customs.

The attendance of both Catholic and Protestant men at the retreat was a testament to these changes. Since the late forties and early fifties, Catholic church traditions have changed tremendously, falling more in line with other denominations of the Christian community. I learned that there is now a broad-based charismatic movement within the Catholic church that is Christ-centered and Spirit-filled. The born again experience, previously associated only with Protestant churches, is now encouraged within the realm of Catholicism. Currently, there are fewer differences and more communication among Christian denominations than there were when I was a child.

The Tres Dias experience led me to thoughts about who makes the rules that govern mankind. The men at the retreat put all their faith in the Bible as the true word of God. If the Bible is true, and all men have a sinful nature inherited from their fall from grace in the Garden of Eden, then by what authority can corrupted man create his own standards and invent religious laws? What is the difference between religious traditions which are accepted as the law of individual churches, and the law of God literally taken from the Bible? If man creates religious tradition and then judges his peers by those standards, is he really upholding the word of God or the word of man?

It also occurred to me that all basic civil laws of our government are based on Hebrew scriptures. Amazingly, this is something that I hadn't seriously thought of before. I always thought of our laws as man made. The laws of the United States as presented in the Constitution are, in fact, patterned after the ten commandments.

In some way or other, as a result of the faith of our national forefathers, all of us have been guided by God's laws since our birth as United States citizens. Our currency is inscribed, "In God we trust" and our pledge of allegiance declares "one nation under God." How could I have forgotten that our national commitment is based on Bibical law; that everyone's life is linked to the Bible whether he is a professed believer or not?

As I continued to consider these ideas I recognized that I shouldn't blame myself for my ignorance. The current issues of morality in our country are so far removed from the original intention of our lawgivers, that I wasn't really surprised that I'd forgotten the link. Although I didn't consider myself immoral, I knew that I was still greatly influenced by current anti-biblical popular trends. I followed this line of thinking further. I concluded that our jails are filled because we are sinning against God's laws as they are incorporated into our civil law. On the other hand, if we all obeyed them, no one would be in jail at all. If God really did exist, and He gave us the privilege of choosing the course of our own behavior, then it's obvious that we have to choose to abide by His law in order to conform our wills to obey the law of our country.

I'm sure that this simple philosophy has always been recognized easily by most people, but it had completely eluded my conscious mind until that moment. It's easy for anyone to forget the religious intent and vision of our Constitution in light of the pleasures offered by a secular world. Anyway, it was shocking to note how far our nation has drifted from our founder's plan of being a moral nation under God.

I was even more upset to realize how little thought I'd given to any of these issues before. The retreat weekend, which I'd thought of as a nuisance, had proven to be very stimulating. I hadn't expected it to have any impact on my thinking at all. I was actually thankful that my brother coerced me into going.

Yet, my absorption with the questions provoked by my attendance were quickly replaced by the easy going patterns of my normal routine. After all, I was a happy-go-lucky kind of guy. That was the image I had always projected. God stuff was serious. Within a month, I hardly remembered my surprised reaction to the testimonies I'd heard. Gloria's repeated probing questions about my weekend received lukewarm answers. "It was O.K." and "I had fun" were not the responses she wanted. I felt that both she and my brother were trying to coax me into some kind of religious commitment that I was not willing to make.

Almost a year would pass before I would try to remember what I'd learned about prayer. It would take circumstances that left me feeling powerless to create my own personal need to look for the answers that only God would provide.

### Gloria's comments

*I have decided to include a few words about my personal impressions of Bob as he appeared to me at the time he attended the religious retreat in 1989. This was a man who was on everyone's list of favorite people, good natured, witty and ready to joke around at any moment.*

*Slightly naive and eager to please, Bob was the first person to stop the car to break up a neighborhood fight. Good looking, smart and affectionate, he was a great companion. Lazing in a haze of cigarette smoke, waiting and ready for the next competitive card game, Bob made sure he lived every moment of his waking life. The words egotistic, uncaring, rude or the like, could never be applied to him, except of course, when we were in a heated personal argument. But, after all, isn't that every wife's complaint?*

*How did Bob appear to me after the Tres Dias weekend? I could easily check off "all of the above." I'd purchased an easy to read* Good News *Bible for him, since he seemed to equate the "thee" and "thou" of the King James version with the outdatedness of Bibical truths. He started to read it, but then quickly lost interest. He refused to discuss the weekend with me, leading me to believe it had not impressed him.*

*I was very discouraged about Bob not developing a relationship with the Lord. I worried about his salvation. But, I reasoned, Bob was such a delightful person to be with, and so good to others that I just had to believe that God had touched him in some way.*

*On another deeper level, I was concerned that Bob was a little too lighthearted. I had survived a difficult youth, and my adult viewpoints were colored with memories of the emotional battles I'd fought. Bob, on the other hand, was seemingly unscarred. He behaved as if he had never experienced a bad day in his life. I began to believe his emotional depth was shallow and I sensed an emptiness in him that made me uncomfortable. I prayed for him and our relationship. I did not want any*

19

unresolved differences between us. I wanted unity in our spiritual lives.

I prayed that the Lord would open his eyes with a dose of reality. This world is filled with misery, yet my husband acted as if nothing bothered him. He laughed everything off. He did not know when people were taking advantage of him. I was afraid that Bob would never turn to God because he would never recognize that he needed Him. I begged the Lord to shake Bob up and open his eyes. If a weekend filled with Christian love would not do it, if reading the Bible would not do it, then I would have to rely solely on God Himself to accomplish it.

# Chapter 3

## When a Nobody Talks to God

Bob's first journal entry
April, 1990

I am a nobody. I am not unique. In spite of inflated egos, no one is really special. Wealth, position, fame or the lack of it, doesn't make any one person different from another. Distinctions of color, ethnic backgrounds, geographical locations do not matter. We are all nobodies, little specks of matter in our vast complicated world.

We each have limited control over the small area of our influence, but in the long run, all our lives are dictated by the finite parameters of birth and death. By those standards, none of us receives special treatment. No one can escape the reality of the advancement of energetic youth to creaky old age. Each of us must face disappointment, frustration, illness, and loss of love, regardless of our race, culture, financial position or level of personal success. It's almost impossible to live a full life without having some bitter experience in relationships with our fellow man.

Personal conflicts and discontents are dwarfed by the larger, criminally damaging wars of nations. Violence and the threat of destruction invade all of our lives. Although we wish it otherwise, the progress of modern technology, while providing improved conveniences and new cures for disease, shares its advances with the development of bigger and better offensive weapons of war. As individuals, we feel helplessly exposed to a tidal wave of new threats against our freedom to pursue a simple peaceful life. People would have to entirely ignore the radio, television and most printed materials to maintain a feeling of well being; assuming all other elements for a happy life were already in place. Governments call the shots. Domestic politics are affected by international financial liaisons and the rules governing all societies are being altered.

Even though I'm aware of the frustrations of modern society, I have never been particularly unhappy with the image of being a nobody. I've been comfortable with the picture of being a nice happy average kind of guy. Gloria and I have a good marriage. Our being together twenty-four hours a day for the last fifteen years and the advantage of our mutual self-employment have forged a friendship and happy dependency between us. My daughter Valerie recently made a comment that we are "joined at the hip." I like that picture. We are really bonded to one another.

We sell antiques for a living. It's not a financially

predicable profession. We travel to antique shows offering items for sale from our collection of Oriental antiques. All the money that we make, aside from bill paying, is reinvested in our business. If we have a succession of bad shows, we go into hock; that is, we extend ourselves into the overdraft reserve of our checkbook and live off that money until the business turns around and we can repay it. We have no savings or retirement accounts. I have no life insurance. But, considering that we had five children to support, a house to maintain located in one of the highest taxed counties of the nation, and no guaranteed income to count on, I think we've done pretty well. Gloria says our life is dominated by financial pressures. I don't like to feel that way, so I leave the task of paying bills to her.

I've always enjoyed working. The challenge of making a living on my own excites me. I never liked getting lost in the crowd of a large corporation. The predictability of a nine to five job bores me. I'm a smoker, a nail biter and a gum chewer. Although I'm aware that these are standard indicators of a nervous personality, I have never openly acknowledged any conscious anxiety or worry in my life.

Gloria says I'm an optimistic gambler in life, but I say that I just have the confidence to get things done. She claims that I am too self-deterministic and that I deny stress. She insists that our life would improve in all ways if I would surrender my will to God as she has done. I've replied to her that I'm an ordinary guy, a nobody, a self-sufficient, happy enough nobody.

But now, as I transfer my thoughts to paper, I can honestly reveal for the first time that I am, in fact, a self deceiving liar. The disappointments and frustrations I've faced in recent years have taught me a lesson in facing reality. I am really not in control of my life. Many times, I feel lost because I can't help my precious daughter Regina, who has been diagnosed as depressed and suicidal and is now confined to a public mental hospital. I cannot allow myself to consciously think about the fact that all three of my children were badly mistreated by my ex-wife's husband. I feel angry about all the years I was prevented from seeing them by their mother's obstinacy, or their stepfather's interference with my visitation. I am tired of the expensive court battles and injustices.

I feel physical pain at the thought of the atrocities inflicted upon my children by their surrogate father, who was punished only in a perfunctory way by the court system. On March 8, 1988 he implicated himself in a taped telephone conversation and was subsequently arrested and charged with counts of rape, sodomy and sexual abuse. On March 23, 1988 my ex-wife filed an unopposed permanent order of protection against him stating that he had been indicted for sexually abusing one, and possibly two, of her daughters. I hate the court's acceptance of plea bargaining which makes it possible to reduce a confessed rapist's crimes to abuse and neglect.

To receive justice, all three of my children would have had to testify in a trial that would have further scarred them. Regina had already run away and had been placed in a protected environment. Instead of a trial, his punishment was determined by a hearing, where with the help of a top notch lawyer, he pleaded guilty only to the reduced charges of attempted rape and sexual abuse. The short amount of time he spent in jail and his limited parole can never pay for the permanent psychological damage he's done to my children. The sexual abuse of my girls, the physical and verbal abuse of my son, my ex-wife's struggles to repair her life after she faced these vile occurrences and events, has left me feeling helpless and despairing.

I cannot erase any of the damage that's been done. My smiles are wearing thin. Gloria only has hints of my pain. I am a convincing liar in my refusal to relay my hurt to her, and most of the time, I'm quite adept at lying to myself as well. Yet, tonight I am suffering, alone and in secret. I'm like the soldier in the fox hole reaching out in desperation. I am under a bombardment of disillusionment. Life is not what I expected. I remember now the personal stories of pain I heard at the religious retreat.

"God, if you are there and if You can hear the prayers of a skeptical nobody, then here I am. I confess my prayers are said without full confidence of being heard. I am doubtful, but I want You to really be there. I am needy. No one, not even my wife, can soothe the hurt that I am hiding from the world. I can hardly acknowledge it myself. If you hear me, Jesus, please answer me so I can believe in something stronger than myself. Release me from my burdens and sins. Heal my sick child. Help me to find a secure financial future for my family.      Amen"

I've decided to keep writing a journal for a while. It feels good to confess my feelings, even if it's just to a piece of paper. I need a record of my thoughts and experiences. It's really an experiment for me to write at all. I'm not sure if I'm going to be happy with the outcome. I feel that I have already revealed more of myself to this piece of paper than I have ever consciously admitted to myself in silent thought. I embarrass myself with my own vulnerability. I guess it doesn't really matter because I will probably end up throwing this notebook away.

I am suddenly afraid of not having my prayers answered. Does this mean that I really have had some kind of subliminal faith all along, which I've kept from emerging for fear of disappointment? Have I been keeping God as my ace-in-the-hole without realizing it, to be pulled out in case things get tough? Did the routine prayers spoken in my childhood really establish a relationship with God that He acknowledged and I forgot? Or, is Gloria's influence and my brother's enthusiastic born again preaching affecting my independent rational thought, which normally places a supernatural God in the same category as the fictional "Twilight Zone"?

What is the voice that directs the lives of believers? What does it sound like? Is it like the earthquake rumbling depicted in Hollywood movies, or is it like a whisper that no one else can hear? I've never had the interest in knowing before. I don't have the nerve to ask anyone now. I will have to find out for myself. Of one thing I am sure, I will keep an accurate record of any answers that I get, that is, if I get any at all. If there really are any answers to prayer, I don't want to miss the connection, so I will continue to make entries in this journal for a while to see what happens.

## Gloria's comments

*Regina, Bob's younger daughter, re-entered our lives after a seven year separation when she was a fifteen year old inmate in Sagamore Children's Hospital, a psychiatric facility for problem children on Long Island. Months later, we would discover that she was admitted to the hospital after a suicide attempt.*

*She'd written Bob a letter, pleading for him to come to see her, saying that she needed her real daddy. When he first saw her name on the return address of the letter, we were standing next to the mail box at the curb in front of our house. Bob opened the envelope immediately.*

*Grabbing my arm and steering me right back to the car we'd just left, Bob drove directly to the hospital, forgetting our dinner and all our other commitments that evening. I was delighted with Bob's reaction. The glow of excitement he was feeling radiated from his whole body. We had no way of determining that we were headed towards a psychiatric facility from the address on the envelope. Bob and I both assumed that we would obtain a hospital pass and see Regina that evening.*

*Our joy was quickly extinguished, however, when we got to the hospital. We were not allowed to visit with Regina, not that night or any other time for many months to come. Regina's visitation was restricted. Bob's ex-wife, who retained sole custody of his children, had* succeeded in putting a ban on any visits but her own. We went back many times after that in the following months, only to be told that the ban was still in effect despite Regina's many letters of request.

Three months later, armed with a folder full of her letters, we parked ourselves in the hospital lobby ready for a sit-in demonstration when Bob had an inspired thought. He called the hospital director and told him that we had the local newspaper and t.v. station on call to come down if we did not get to see his daughter that day. Within one hour, Bob was granted his first visit with his daughter in seven years. From Regina's positive reaction to seeing her father, the hospital agreed to allow both of us one supervised visit a week. Over the next two months Regina filled in some of the details of her life during the years we had missed.

We already knew that a learning disability was suspected by her teachers when she was in first grade because we were still in contact at that time. But there was much we did not know. By third or fourth grade she was labeled as dyslexic and had to repeat a term in school. She had become a behavior problem as well. Acting out in class was her solution to the academic frustration that she faced each day. Finally, she was removed from the general school population and sent to a special school for children with learning disabilities. She'd been in and out of institutions from the time she was eleven years old.

In addition to these problems, she had to cope with the divorce of her parents, the abusive sexual perversions of her stepfather who threatened her mother's death if Regina ever revealed the truth, and the failure of the court system to enforce Bob's visitation, (which would have allowed her visits with a healthy family). Her resolve to live was exhausted along with her feelings of self worth. Her saving graces, if not academic, were her common sense, her sweet and loving disposition, and her very pretty face.

Many of the teachers and hospital attendants who cared for her were moved to tears by the obvious concern she showed for others. She was insightful, empathetic and cared deeply for the welfare of other patients.

One day we were denied visitation because we were told that Regina was being punished for attacking an eleven year old girl. We were ready to scold her on our next visit until we saw the girl. She must have been one of the biggest eleven year olds on earth. She stood 5'7" tall and weighed in at over 150 pounds. Regina was 4' 10" and about 105 pounds at that time. Despite her small stature, when Regina was angry she had immense, fearless strength. Several attendants had nicknamed her "Rambo." One of the staff told us that Regina jumped on the bigger girl because she was literally sitting on top of another child lying beneath her on the floor. In an attempt to help her friend, she attacked the oversized girl.

She knew that she would be punished for her actions, but she chose to protect someone who was too weak to defend herself. Regina thought nothing of sacrificing herself for others. Yet, she allowed herself no self pity, and was filled with self-contempt for her own body and mind.

When she had bouts of self-hatred, she often went into rages and the hospital staff would subdue her. One of the attendants, a big burly fellow, told us that when the alarm bell rang on her floor, he rushed to get there before anyone else to see if Regina was in trouble. He was concerned that she would be handled too roughly by the others and he knew how to overpower her without hurting her. He also tried to intervene to keep the nurses from using a straight jacket. If he could get her into a "quiet room" quickly, she would get a sedative rather than be bound.

Bob and I were completely unaware of her problems through the years, because all three of his children had been physically and psychologically removed from our lives by their stepfather. The children were persuaded that Bob was uninterested in their welfare and that he had never loved them. Bob and I battled the court system for visitation until there was no fight left in us. We were mentally and financially depleted. The children had been brainwashed and reprogrammed. They did not want to see their father. He was the bad guy.

Bob always maintained that Regina would be the first of his children to make contact with him someday. He considered her to be his "special" child. Using the knowledge he had gained from his Navy hospital corps training as a medic, Bob had suspected that she was born with learning disabilities that were not easily diagnosed in her first few years of life. Regina's story verified that his early suspicions were accurate. Also, she did not have the strong constitution that Valerie, her older adopted sister possessed. Valerie was a fighter. She'd managed to intellectualize her abuse and go on to lead a productive life.

As we proceeded to learn more about Regina's life, we were saddened to discover that by the time she was *eleven years old she had become a truant from school and had begun to resort to alcohol and drugs as an escape from her reality. Running away and prostitution followed. She had an abortion. Her intellect was affected by all the toxic substances and she began to hallucinate and hear voices. All the horrors of an abnormal mind became her reality.*

*When we finally became part of her life again, Bob became her lifeline. His love for her was filled with unrestrained compassion and tenderness. She considered our house her home away from hospital settings, although she also spent time with Bob's brother Ray and her maternal uncle Richard. She was very resourceful in her choice of hospitals. Uncle Richie lived in New Orleans and anytime Regina had an urge to see Mardi Gras she would check herself in at a hospital near him. He was as devoted to helping her as we were.*

*We realized over time that she was much smarter than her school records indicated. Her stepfather had insisted that all her behavior problems including her dyslexia had been inherited from her father. When she was a teenager just getting to know her dad again, she discovered that there were plenty of good things that she had inherited from him. She did share Bob's dyslexia, but just like him, she was bright and clever when it came to getting things that she wanted.*

*She also exhibited good reasoning power and strong common sense. One day when the three of us were together, she chastised Bob for the way he spoke to me. She complained that he picked on me for small things. Bob answered by telling her that I understood that he was just teasing me about something insignificant. He then went on to tell her a story about the time I knocked over and broke the most valuable antique in our shop. It was a large floor vase that I backed into as I rose from bending over to pick something up. It smashed to the floor and shattered irreparably when it toppled over.*

*Bob told Regina that he did not say one bad word to me after the vase was broken. "Why didn't I pick on her then?" he asked Regina. She answered almost immediately, "You couldn't yell at her then because you knew how bad she was feeling inside. You knew that she was punishing herself already, so you didn't have the heart to say anything more about it."*

*We discovered she had also inherited Bob's sense of humor. When she came home to stay with us from one of her recurrent Louisiana sojourns, she criticized Bob for driving too fast. "Hey Dad," she shouted out over the noise of the road, the tapping of her hands on the dashboard keeping time to the rock music she had blasting out of her stereo earphones, "slow down. I'm not feeling suicidal today."*

*Our family tried to rebuild her delicate psyche through love and a stable home life. Bob spent his every waking hour with her when she was with us. Nevertheless, we learned to expect that coming home to stay really meant a temporary visit.*

*But I'm getting way ahead of Bob's journal.*

*At the time of Bob's first journal entry, he was again fighting for the right to visit with Regina. Regina had managed to run away from Sagamore several months earlier. She'd requested that Ray try to obtain legal custody of her so that she would not have to return to the institution. Mr. Gabriel, our attorney, succeeded in getting an immediate court order for temporary custody. We immediately had Regina evaluated by a psychiatrist who encouraged her to begin private therapy.*

*The judicial order was rescinded five days later, just before her first session. The judge discovered that Regina was no longer in her mother's custody but had been temporarily made a ward of the state. Mr. Gabriel explained that the F.B.I was on its way to pick her up and that we all would be accused of kidnapping if she was found in Ray's house.*

*I answered the frantic telephone call from the lawyer. He told me not to allow her to return to Ray's house, but to ask her to turn herself in immediately. I was to call him from a certain location with Regina, and he would give me further instructions.*

*My father-in-law acted as a sentry at the street corner in case I missed intercepting Bob and Regina returning to the house. I was sitting in my car one block away hoping to stop Bob before he reached the corner turn. We expected them to be back at any minute.*

*In the car with them were Ray and Joe (one of Bob's close friends who had recently retired from the police force). I succeeded in intercepting the car and, one step short of hysteria, I informed them briefly of the lawyer's call. Regina sent me home for her suitcase while we waited for her decision about what she wanted to do. She decided to return to the hated hospital rather than cause her family trouble with the law. Joe, Bob's police buddy, accompanied the three of us to the phone rendezvous, while Ray took the car home to wait for the expected visit of the government officials. Regina, having fully accepted the idea of her return to the hospital, then thought it very funny to have a policeman help her to flee from FBI arrest.*

*The protocol for her return was outlined by Mr. Gabriel when we called, and we took Regina to be voluntarily readmitted to the hospital. Ray continued his battle to gain custody of her, but the case collapsed when she refused to face her mother in court.*

*Bob was once again blocked from seeing his daughter. This time his ex-wife had managed to secure an official court order to stop his visitation. Ray, his wife Carol and Bob's parents were still allowed weekly visits but Bob's involvement was limited to censored letters and reports from his relatives. He had tried his best to help his daughter get private treatment away from a hospital setting. Not only had the plan failed, but he had also lost visiting privileges.*

*While Bob's frustration was obvious to me, his crying out to God was well hidden. I thought I was praying for help alone.*

Bob's journal continued
Late April 1990

O.K. So I've prayed my prayer. I've asked God to heal my child Regina. This is both a selfish and an unselfish prayer. I've asked God to provide me with more material wealth, definitely a selfish prayer. Several questions have occurred to me. First, why would God want to answer my prayers? How can I tell if it is truly God answering or just a coincidence? What if the answer to prayer is a result of my own positive thinking or just chance?

I know that in the past I've had silent hopeful thoughts that some people might call praying, although they did not represent what I would call a formal prayer. I may even have addressed God, yet it felt more like introspection or free associative thinking to me. I certainly did not have any confidence of these "thought" prayers being heard. I remember asking for my children to contact me after a forced separation of seven years, despite the prohibition of their stepfather. Two years passed before I got Regina's letter from a state hospital. How then, can I know if the letter was a coincidence or an answer from God?

After I started to receive Regina's letters, I prayed for an opportunity to speak with my ex-wife in order to open a line of communication. I specifically asked for a half an hour to one hour conversation. I called her the next day, and for the first time in twelve years, she spoke to me. To say that I put up with a barrage of verbal abuse is an understatement, but my purpose was to convince her to allow me visitation rights to see Regina in the hospital. The phone call lasted forty-five minutes. She vented her emotions and I listened with forced patience. She did not grant permission, but when I finally circumvented the hospital red tape by threatening negative publicity and was finally allowed to see Regina, Ann my ex-wife, stopped objecting to my visits. If it were not for that prior phone call, I am sure Ann would have fought hard and long to prevent me from seeing her. It left the lines of communication open.

Was my own positive thinking on the day that I called the catalyst for "breaking the ice," or was it God acting in my life, giving me a positive answer to my request within twenty-four hours of it being made? At the time it definitely felt like a prayer was being answered.

It has been nine months since I went on the retreat, but it's only now that I can admit that I really would like to believe in all the things that my brother and his Christian friends believe. I would like to be sure that God really exists as the creator of this world and all that's in it. I would like to know Him as a caring and loving father to His children. I would like to think that I have the right to pray to Him and get an answer. But, how do I get around my skepticism? Doubting Thomas was an amateur compared to me.

If my current prayers are not answered, however, does that mean that He really does not exist and I am willfully or wishfully deceiving myself with the reasoning of deluded Christians? Or, are unanswered prayers, assuming they are heard, unanswered because it's not the right time, not the right reason, not the right prayer? Maybe we haven't prayed hard enough, we are not deserving, or even, that God has changed his mind? What am I saying? Am I making excuses for God not answering me? Am I trying to rationalize that God might be there even if I don't get any personal messages from Him?

I'm starting to address Biblical questions to my brother Ray and my wife Gloria, but I'm doing it in a way to discourage any thoughts about my personal needs. They don't even suspect that my questions are anything but gibes. I make it seem that I'm teasing them about their blind faith. If I casually make any reference to God, Gloria and Ray fall all over themselves to give me information. If I answer their attempts to convince me in any negative way, they run to get a Bible to support their conversation. They both have repeatedly quoted from the Bible, indicating all prayer be directed through Jesus. They have coaxed me to read the book of John.

At Gloria's insistence, I have attempted to read the Bible several times before. Since it is customary to start a book on its first page, I began reading the Old Testament. By the time I got through the first few books I felt like I was in the middle of a science fiction movie. The stories seem unreal to me. Noah and his ark, Jonah and the whale remind me of fairy tales. Gloria suggests I feel this way because I am reading it as a novel and not as the word of God.

Now I've been advised to read a chapter from the New Testament. Four verses from the book of John, that quote Jesus' words, stand out in my mind.

..."I am the way, and the truth, and the life; no one comes to the Father, but through me." (John 14:6)

"Do you not believe that I am in the Father, and the Father is in Me? The words that I say to you I do not speak on My own initiative, but the Father abiding in Me, does His works." (John 14:10)

"And whatever you ask in My name, that will I do, that the Father may be glorified in the Son." (John 14:13)

"If you ask Me anything in My name, I will do it." (John 14:14).

Well, it seems that I have been doing things wrong again. I have been praying to the Father without acknowledging the Son. I would think, however, that God would be smart enough to know my intention without all the formalities. Yet, Jesus is very clear about the protocols for successful prayer. Who am I to say He is wrong? I'm more worried about the content of my prayers than the way they are said. After reading John I still think my prayers are selfish, and that God, if He is really there, will think they are self-serving.

I can't imagine God listening to me anyway, but I will continue to pray in hope, for Regina's sake.

She is not doing at all well in the hospital. She has been on suicide watch all week. I was finally allowed to talk to her on the phone today and she sounded awful. I don't know if it's the drugs that are slowing her down, or if she is still depressed.

It was a real coincidence to hear Gloria say today that we are "nobody" without God. My point exactly, but with a substantial modification. The implication is that with God we are somebody, a point that I have never acknowledged. But, if God is truly our Father, I am but one of a multitude of children, and like a child in a very large family I feel lost in the crowd. Yet, as a parent and step-parent I know that in my combined brood of five, I love each child separately and distinctly from the other.

This leads me to think of how He might still hear my voice in the many prayers that are addressed to Him. It becomes a feasible thought then, that with a true faith in

God, I could become a somebody. But, I am once again assailed with doubts that I can personally have such a faith, even though I have seen evidence of it at the retreat and in the lives of other family members. If my prayers go unanswered, I doubt that I will believe at all. It's not like I am praying for world peace, or the end to famine or other such noble ideals. I certainly am not a Billy Graham. My prayers are admittedly selfish. Yet, from the standpoint of being a father, I know that many times my children's requests are selfish, and that does not necessarily mean that they are wrong.

As a parent I have to decide which requests to grant and which to refuse. If I can see a just reason for any request and I can satisfy a need, I will go out of my way to grant it because I love my children and will try to please them. As a father, I will discern the value of each and every one of my children's requests and favor them unless there is a good reason not to do so. If I refuse, it's because I know that granting such requests will be detrimental to them in some way. If I have to say no, it will be to protect them. My sternness at times might make one of them feel unloved at the moment, but my decision is always made out of love. In the long run I expect them to know this. I expect, that in time, they will know my values and will not make requests which they know in advance will be rejected.

It follows then, if I am a child of God, that perhaps it is possible that my Father will grant my requests. This line of thinking has made me feel a lot better about my prayers. I don't think, at this moment, that my prayers will go unanswered, even if the answer is no. What I still lack is the absolute proof that God is listening and considering my petitions.

I have forgotten an important point. When children want something badly, often they will offer to barter for it. In exchange for a parent granting their desire, they may promise to do something in return that will please their mom or dad. I think I will approach my prayer in a different way.

If I, a skeptic, a doubtful believer, have my prayers answered in a tangible way, I promise God that I will then acknowledge Him as the answer to my good fortune. I will praise Him publicly. I will openly admit to the source of my faith and feel free to tell the world about it. Gloria and I will write a book about how a skeptic's prayers were answered by God. What better bargain from a skeptic can God get?

## Gloria's comments

*I was delighted to see my husband follow up on Ray's suggestion that he read the book of John in the New Testament. I felt sure that Bob would be impressed when he read the words that were so enlightening to me in my personal search for truth. Although I was entirely unaware of Bob's journal, I sensed that he was genuinely curious about God in a personal way. I knew, that beneath his exterior nonchalance, he had suffered terribly from his separation from his children, but that he would never verbally divulge his pain to me. It just wasn't part of his machismo.*

*Although I had spoken about my faith for years, he would not reveal his personal thoughts about God to me. I had prayed for him to become a believer. I had* faith that God would comfort him if he would only open the door. I'd prayed for a miracle that would bring back the affection of all three of his children. I'd asked that his former wife's heart would be softened and open to our communication so we could participate together in the children's' lives as an extended family.

Looking back from my current perspective, it seems that God's positive answers to my prayers depended entirely upon His acceptance of the bargain that Bob made with Him in this early entry of his journal. If God had answered my prayers any earlier, how would Bob have ever discovered that the reply came from Him? He would have assumed that his good luck was just the result of chance and taken the renewed relationship with his children for granted. Would he have believed me if I stated that I felt that the reunification of our family was connected to my personal petitions to God? Surely he would have thought it was all coincidence.

Bob's prayer for faith depended upon God revealing Himself in clearly discernible ways. Otherwise, he was unwilling to give up his skepticism. By bargaining, Bob challenged God to prove His existence. When God responded to Bob's bargain by providing proof, the evidence was oftentimes an answer to my earlier requests.

God's ways are a mystery to us. Here we are, weak and needy human beings, all praying to God in our personal solitude. How can we know if our prayer requests are linked to events in other people's lives? What is God's timetable for answering the call of believers? The events of one person's life may be linked to the prayers of a complete stranger. Events may have to fall into God's preordained sequence before He chooses to *coax the first domino to fall. My request could be at the very end of the wave. We cannot see the big picture that God already knows. In our case my prayers came first, but Bob's had to be answered before mine could be. My answers were linked to Bob's acceptance of God. Who can explain how God fits the pieces of such a complex puzzle together?*

*How much proof did Bob need to be sure of God's Presence? Lots and lots of evidence, over and over again.*

*Was my own faith challenged along the way? Yes, it certainly was!*

*Did I anticipate that I was going to write a book to glorify God? Never in my wildest dreams!*

*Do God's ends justify the means? Yes, and yes again, if the end is unwavering faith, the promise of eternal life and the glorification of His name.*

# Chapter 4

## When God Talks to a Nobody

Bob's journal continued
May 14th 1990

Gloria and I were headed west to Kansas City to sell at an antique show. I was chain smoking my way through the tedious trip on the Pennsylvania Turnpike. As I reached into my left shirt pocket for another cigarette, Gloria handed me a lollipop and suggested that I take it instead of the cigarette that I planned to smoke. I hate being told not to smoke by anybody, so I took the lollipop in my right hand and attempted to toss it out through my window. That would teach her to stop bugging me about my smoking! I'd forgotten that the window was closed. The lollipop bounced back and ended up on my lap. Too lazy to roll down the window, I reconsidered, and put it into my mouth instead.

It may sound ridiculous to say that at the moment of

this simple and insignificant act, a life changing event took place. But that was the moment that God chose to let me know that He really was there and that my prayers would be answered.

God chose that moment in time to speak to me. I knew His voice. I would be tempted to think that it was a subliminal thought breaking through to consciousness, but the idea that came to me from God, literally from out of the blue, was recognized by my mind as not being mine.

The clearest way to explain it is as follows: if I imagine my wife or friend is talking to me I absorb that imagined conversation in my mind with the outwardly silent but inwardly audible and familiar voice of the person who is speaking; if I am thinking of a conversation that took place between my wife and my friend, I can distinguish who is saying what by the sound of their voice in my thoughts. In the same vein, when we are dreaming we "hear" what is going on in our dreams. Apparently, our minds can reproduce sounds in our memories, without the necessity of having our auditory nerves stimulated. I was about to hear a new voice.

What happened at that moment in my truck? I had an idea. The exact idea that was presented in my mind was, "if the lollipop in my mouth had nicotine in it, I would not need to smoke another cigarette." As I had that idea, I heard an inner voice, one that I did not recognize as any I had heard before. The voice said, "This is for you." The voice also said, "This will change your life and answer your prayers." At that moment, I knew with certainty, that the idea that flashed into my thoughts without premeditation had come from God. I knew that it was going to change my destiny.

I turned to Gloria and said, "This is it. I've got it. I have an idea that will make us millionaires." I then told her about the idea of a nicotine lollipop. I didn't tell her that the idea had come from the Lord. She didn't know that I had a prayer life. I don't know why I haven't chosen to tell her, but I don't feel comfortable sharing this religious experience with her for fear she would think that I've gone crazy. She doesn't know I have been petitioning God for changes in my life. How could I explain this to her? Also, I imagine there may still be some skepticism in me and I don't want to share anything I'm not sure of. And yet, even though my head is trying to tell me this is my idea, my heart keeps assuring me that the idea came directly from God and was not my own.

Gloria didn't respond with any enthusiasm. She knew about many ideas and projects that I'd attempted in the past without any financial rewards. As a matter of fact, most of them cost me money instead of earning additional income. She couldn't understand my excitement. Before she could even give me her opinion, I told her of my plans to see a patent attorney. I talked about sharing our wealth with friends and family, and about how useful the money would be in getting Regina proper psychiatric help. I could see by her response to what she must have first thought to be manic ramblings that she was thoughtfully analyzing the reasons for my excitement.

During the next three days at the antique show, we were pretty much occupied with our business and busy socializing with other antique dealers after show hours.

We didn't talk much about the project. I had already concluded that my next step was to hire a patent lawyer. I was anxious to proceed to carry out God's plan.

I, as a nobody, have offered myself to God as a witness for Him in return for an answer to prayer. I was wrong in thinking that no one can be a somebody. God Himself has seen fit to change me into a somebody, in order to enact my testimony.

It feels great to be a somebody. It's going to be fun getting started on a new project. I'm full of wonder about this miracle that is taking place, that God could step into my life in one tiny second and change my future. I am somebody because God has spoken to me. I am filled with joy, but at the same time I am humbled by the power of the Almighty. My eyes are tearing at the thought that He could care so much about me. Now I can identify with the men at the retreat. They shed tears of gratitude to the same loving God who saves us from our worldly circumstance and gives us hope.

## Gloria's comments

*When Bob turned to me in the truck and told me he had an idea that was going to make us millionaires, I thought, "Oh no, not another one." I'd heard lots of teasing about his past ventures as an entrepreneur. His track record since we'd been together also revealed several creative endeavors gone bad. His ideas were not off-the-wall notions, but inevitably they did not work out. I was in no mood for another failure. We had enough financial responsibility without creating further debts by investing money recklessly. But, during the trip home, as Bob kept pointing out the merits of a product that would satisfy a smoker's habit in a non-smoking environment, I started to see its usefulness to society. We began a brainstorming session that lasted through the long trip home. I even contributed a name for the product. It would be called "Nic Stics."*

*I found a lawyer who referred us to a patent attorney. While we were waiting for an appointment, Bob was talking about Nic Stics to our close friends and family, despite my protests that there was no point in getting people excited about an idea that might not be patentable. Regardless of my cooperation on the trip home, I was really not convinced that the idea could be patented. Nicorette Gum and the patch were already on the market. Would a lollipop have more appeal to a smoker than either of these products?*

*Bob insisted that oral gratification was the key appeal and that the other products were inferior to his idea because they did not deal with the oral compulsive behavior that was linked to smoking. Nic Stics could be put in and out of the mouth like a cigarette and sucking was similar to inhaling. The shape of the lollipop would resemble a cigarette and the packaging would look like a cigarette pack.*

*Bob not only spoke about Nic Stics, he actually persuaded our friends and family to invest in the patent process. He possesses the wonderful ability to convey his enthusiasm and generate an equal response in a listener. His motivation was not prompted by a need for money. We had enough to get the process started ourselves. He really wanted his friends to be involved and enjoy his experience with him. For a few hundred dollars they would have a vested interest in all the fun. Also, he really wanted to share the income he expected to get from the invention. Bob is a very generous person.*

*The fact that people really love my husband was verified by the fact that everyone he asked gave him some money for a share of a patent that was still just a dream. At least that was all I thought it was at the time. Getting friends involved also insured that he would always have someone to talk to, and talk he did ... and did... and did. I had never heard him so enthusiastic before.*

*We finally went to our free consultation with the patent attorney the following week. It was no surprise to me that the lawyer was not any more optimistic than I was. He warned us that attempting to get a patent was costly. Bob pushed him for a percentage of estimated success. He did not give the idea more than a 3% chance of being passed. Bob, with his characteristic optimism, said that 3% was good enough for him. Inwardly, he was thinking that what was promised by the Lord could not be thwarted by a mere 97% handicap. He took out our check book and told the lawyer to "go for it."*

*I could not understand where Bob's confidence came from. I was intimidated by the lawyer's pessimism. If an attorney who was reputed to be a genius at getting patents for his clients didn't believe it was a good idea, I was not going to get my hopes up at all. I went home feeling satisfied that our investment would be limited to a patent search and then abandoned.*

*The only benefit I saw in the project, was that it would distract Bob's mind from Regina's illness. It was worth the effort for that reason alone. I would help him face the disappointment of not getting a patent when the time came. Until then I would pretend to share his enthusiasm.*

*Bob was right. If he had told me that his idea had come straight from God at that time, I really would have thought he was crazy. The God I knew would never come up with such a wacky idea. Looking back, I have to laugh at my concept. The Lord is not in the business of making false promises. He did have a purpose in mind and He was leading us right down a path He had already paved. We would have to have patience and discernment to follow it. We would travel it in darkness, not seeing exactly where we were being led. Bob was going to step off the road into thorny bushes many times. Eventually, we would get to our destination, but it would take a few years to get there.*

Bob's journal continued
June 20, 1990

I guess my friends and family think I've flipped. All my thoughts and conversations revolve around Nic Stics. They don't understand why I am so confident. Gloria can't understand it either. They all are waiting for the results of the patent search, probably with the idea of kidding me mercilessly when the lawyer delivers his bad news. I guess I have justly earned a reputation for good but non-profitable ideas.

Gloria's attitude has been kind of neutral. I think she is trying not to hurt my feelings while she anticipates a future disappointment for me. Basically, I'm not concerned about what anyone thinks. I'm just waiting to hear from the lawyer. I am sure that his news will confirm God's plan that we go ahead and file for a patent. I just can't wait to get this project started!

June 26, 1990

I am so impatient that I called the attorney today. The patent search is still in progress. He hasn't received any news yet. He told me he heard a commercial for a new non-smoking device on the radio today. I am going to start scanning the channels to find that commercial. It's amazing that I started to have negative thoughts as soon as I heard this news.

Was this our lawyer's way of trying to tell me that it is impossible to get the patent? I'm starting to think about how I will feel if this doesn't work out. How can I think this way? As I think back, it seems to me that God had a hand in bringing all three of my children back into my life. I believe that He is answering my prayers. I certainly believe that He personally spoke to me when He gave me the idea for Nic Stics. One negative fact comes up, and I find myself suddenly doubting. Is my new found faith already failing?

4:45 p.m.

Suddenly, in the middle of this negative thought, comes a silent voice in my mind, spoken with authority, spoken from outside my own thoughts. It says, "Why do you doubt Me?", and I am immediately humbled in the presence of Almighty God. It is happening again, as I write in this diary. Once again I feel His presence in my mind and I recognize Him.

June 27, 1990
10:15 a.m.

Well, I just mailed away for the new smoking devise that was advertised on the radio. Now it is just a matter of waiting to see if it contains candy. I can't believe that I still have some doubts about Nic Stics going through, despite my 100% faith when the idea presented itself and the confirmation from the Lord that I received yesterday.

I had been praying for a career change and it seemed that my prayers were answered in an even more amazing way than I ever could have expected. For the first time in my life I felt I knew God. Now, because I am restless for news from the patent office, and because of the radio commercial, I feel my faith starting to fail. I don't want that to happen.

My thoughts are changing focus now. While I am writing this, I am thinking of reasons why God might think it best for this whole plan not to happen. I wish I could just relax. My nerves are on edge. I argued with Gloria and my stepdaughter today and did some other things that I'm sorry about. My thinking is very confused. As soon as I heard about the new anti-smoking devise my doubts became foremost in my thoughts. How can this be? It was only yesterday afternoon that God Himself told me not to doubt Him. What is wrong with me?

June 30, 1990

As my mind wandered during a television commercial tonight, the Lord spoke to me again. He said "Do not doubt; do not worry." Immediately, I was both awed and calmed with this reassurance. Nevertheless, even now as I write, my mind keeps wondering about when we will get an answer from the lawyer. My everyday, unspiritual mind still needs a confirmation that this idea is not just a flight of fancy.

July 7, 1990

No news. Maybe Nic Stics is only a bridge to something else. Maybe the only reason that this idea happened is because God wants me to write a book on prayer. I just can't ignore the intense feeling I have that God has plans for me. Why me? I've stopped playing lotto, because I no longer feel that there is a need to hope for sudden fortune. Is it realistic to feel that I have a 95% chance of my invention becoming a reality? Why 95%?

Why at other times do I feel that if this doesn't work I'll have to devise some other plan? When I consider my faith, I feel like I'm on a roller coaster. What if I just attempt to stop thinking about all this and just wait and see what happens? But, I can't let myself do this because that would be like leaving God out of it. Should I continue to pray each day for a successful outcome with the patent office, or shall I rest in the fact that this prayer of mine has already been answered and that I should go on and keep my day to day contact with the Lord on other issues?

I am also thinking of the possibility that my actions may change God's mind about everything, or that maybe some forgotten sin from my past, for which I have not repented, will be held against me. All these thoughts reveal my doubts, which at times seem like superstitious nonsense to me. I have overwhelming guilt because of my questioning. How can I now disbelieve what I thought was a true and meaningful experience with God? What will I think of next with my indecisive faith in His promise?

Is it possible that God forgives us our doubts, or must our faith be unfailing at all times? Maybe some doubt is allowed us because God does not always answer our prayers in exactly the way that they were asked. He can have reasons that are known only to Him. Gloria says she ends her prayers of need with "according to Thy will, Lord." Is this a way people can hedge their bets, so no matter how their prayers are answered they can justify it as God's will? This brings me all the way back to my early suspicions that what seem to be answers could just be chance, coincidence or luck and not God at all.

I am very interested in learning more about the nature of faith. As a result, I have become very skillful in quietly initiating discussions about God when we visit my brother. I always play "devil's advocate" so no one will catch on. I tease Ray by calling him a "holy roller". I challenge him to prove God's existence. I have been getting a terrific education this way. I can always count on Raymond to go to the Bible to search out an answer to the issue at hand. Both he and Carol are well schooled through discipleship classes in their church.

Gloria has also done a lot of Bible study. She has been trying to encourage my curiosity by getting me a copy of

The Book, a simplified translation of the Bible, but I am still having trouble understanding. I can see that she is very happy that I have some questions about the Lord, although she cannot begin to imagine how much has taken place in my private relationship with God. I really would like to talk to her about everything that has happened, but I still feel that I must not reveal anything yet. I have so much to learn about man's relationship to Jesus. I feel that this must be an entirely personal experiment.

I am now forty-seven years old and I've done absolutely nothing in my life to help God. I really wish to be able to help Him. How can a man help God? My desire to have Nic Stics succeed is not really selfish. I have promised the Lord that I will give the money freely to support the work of churches and care for the needy. Gloria's daughters, Cindy and Cheryl, and my older daughter Valerie have been blessed with glorious voices. It is my secret plan to have them join efforts in a singing group I would create, one that would be designed to give the message of God to the general population in an appealing way. Also, I have been reading a lot lately concerning the Dead Sea scrolls. I would like to fund an outreach to Jewish people using evidence from the scrolls that relates to the prophetic messages of Jesus as Messiah.

These endeavors will require a lot of money. Royalties from Nic Stics sales could easily get them going. It suddenly occurs to me, as I write this, that this way of thinking may really represent my attempt to blackmail God. I am so terribly anxious for everything to work out because I am afraid of losing the wonderful feeling of having a true faith. "If I don't succeed in getting the patent approved, will I then doubt Your existence again Lord? Or, do I have enough faith and longing for You to overcome the loss of what I interpret as Your promise? Will I act like a five year old who cries when he doesn't get his candy?

Will I still feel like converting this diary to a book if my rainbow has no pot of gold?"

When will I get some news from our lawyer?

## Gloria's comments

*As I read Bob's notes and prepared them for entry into this book, I found myself amused at the struggle he was going through at that time. To vacillate between complete belief in God's personal message to him and his mind's refusal to accept it revealed his naiveté of the ways God manifests Himself to a believer.*

*Although raised in Judaism without any notion of the Trinity, I became acutely aware of the gift of the Holy Spirit when I first became a believer in Messiah Jesus. I sought and found the quiet Voice who becomes our companion in life when we turn ourselves over to God. I accepted God's indwelling Spirit and His direction without contest from the moment I accepted Jesus. But I was coming from a different place. I already believed in The Father.*

*Bob obviously began to experience a gradual religious conversion that began when he prayed while on the retreat weekend. He did not realize that God had then endowed him with His Presence in a new and tangible way. Accustomed to being the sole manipulator of his decisions, he did not recognize the inner Presence of God that was given to him as a helper. Instead of listening to this inner voice in complete trust, he kept overruling it with thoughts empowered by his willful mind, while God was drawing him closer and closer to making a complete commitment to Him. In this battle to retain his skepticism Bob was to become the ultimate loser, because God had already claimed him as His own. God was allowing Bob to question and doubt so that His impact would be felt all the more when He consistently answered Bob's prayers. He was preparing Bob for a great spiritual victory–one that was designed to include both of us so that we could be united as partners in a secure faith.*

# Chapter 5

## Getting to Know You–Day by Day

Bob's journal continued
July 18, 1990

Well, there is very little doubt that God answers prayer. I'm back up to a solid 95% in faith. We finally heard from the lawyer. The patent search revealed nothing to stand in our way, and we are going ahead and preparing to file for a patent on our smoking substitute.

Our lawyer is still far from optimistic that we have a viable product. He is convinced that an adult would not chose to walk around with a cigarette shaped lollipop in his mouth no matter how desperate his need for nicotine. As a non-smoker, he doesn't understand that smoking is not just an addiction to nicotine, that there are psychological and oral compulsive needs that are also ingrained in the smoking habit. Our product would satisfy both needs in a would-be non smoker.

Once again we were reminded of the expense of the patent application process. Even though our lawyer is trying to discourage us, I am even more confident in God's plan for my future and my optimism is high. We still haven't received the anti-smoking device that I sent for, but reason dictates that it is not candy based or it would have shown up on the patent search.

I haven't prayed much in the last two weeks. I've been preoccupied with the lack of business in our store. We haven't made one sale. It is the first time in our five years at this location that we went completely blank. Nevertheless the Lord really came through for us. We were called in by a friend to conduct a warehouse sale. Our percentage of the profits reached $700.00, just the amount we needed for bill-paying this week.

On the down side, Gloria's older daughter moved back into our house this week after ending a long term relationship. There has been a lot of trouble that Cheryl has finally chosen to tell us about. She has been a victim of abusive behavior and, finally, has broken her resolve to stay. Gloria is happy that her relationship is ending because she believes that the young man is a sociopath and that Cheryl is going to be much better off without him. Maybe Gloria's prayers for her daughter have been answered by the end of this troubled association.

August 3, 1990

Our appointment to sign the formal patent application has been canceled twice by our attorney. I have been praying for patience for quite a while now. Gloria tells me repeatedly that I have no patience at all. Yet, I know that normally I would be ranting and raving about the delays, and this time I am not. I have been very unlike myself in the amount of reserve I've exhibited.

I quote my attorney's comment after the two cancellations: "Thank you for having such patience." Of course this could be coincidence or chance, but I feel that it's God's way of letting me know that He is listening, watching and taking care of me. Anyway, we do have a confirmed appointment with the lawyer this evening.

I am aware that I should be worried about someone stealing the idea of Nic Stics, but since this is God's idea, I figure that I have special protection. As a matter of fact, people are advised not to discuss their ideas with anyone until a formal patent application is filed, but I have been bubbling over with the news to everyone. After all, what human could possibly interfere with God's intentions?

August 5, 1990

We are now on a first name basis with our lawyer. Our appointment with Ed went well. Gloria and I signed the patent application as co-inventors. When Gloria suggested we put in applications for foreign patents as well, I couldn't believe it. This will mean a much larger investment than we anticipated. Gloria must really believe in the product now, because she is much more conservative in spending than I am. She must also have the faith that this money will become available, because we certainly don't have it now. I've had to scrape up some of the $1,500.00 that's required just to get us started with the domestic application. I can only attribute her change in attitude to my consistent enthusiasm and the successful results of the patent search.

August 8, 1990

The new non-smoking devise finally arrived in the mail today. As I had expected, from the reassurance of God's inner voice, it had nothing to do with our patent. It contains no candy or nicotine and is no threat to our patent at all.

Lately I've been feeling that it is God's will that I take care of my fourteen year old son Patrick and my ex-wife. I would like to pay off the mortgage on their house. I also feel led to include Regina in the singing group with the girls. She cannot sing on key but she does play the flute. We can call the group the Three Miracles and an Angel. Despite all her horrendous experiences, she is still a little angel to me.

4:00 a.m.

A few hours ago, I got a telephone message from the police that some one had broken into our store. All they told me was that the back door had been pried open after the alarm wires were cut. They didn't know what had been taken. I was aware that I had left about $5,000.00 dollars worth of jewelry in glass cases that could easily be broken open. As we drove to the store, I had the strong feeling that we had not been robbed. I have been very close to the Lord these last months, talking to Him on a daily basis. I felt that He was watching over me. Because of my feeling of His protection, I was not in a desperate hurry to get to my place of business.

On previous occasions, I'd sped through red lights at illegal speeds just to find that I had responded to a false alarm. In this instance, I knew that the store had been definitely broken into and yet I was calm.

When we arrived, the police explained that the street alarm went off when the door was opened, even though the silent alarm to the police was canceled when the wires were cut. A patrol car just happened to be passing by and heard the siren. As the police pulled up in front of the store, whoever was inside ran out through the back door. By the time they reached the back alley he was gone. The police arrived there at the precise moment to abort the success of the robbery.

Not one piece of our merchandise was taken. I was right. God was protecting us. It's a wonderful feeling to know that I have a dynamic relationship with my Father in heaven. I always thought that things really had to get bad before people could go to God for help. Now I realize that it's just a matter of letting Him help you with your everyday life.

The similarity to my relationship with my own children seems appropriate. My kids speak to me about their lives and I share my opinions with them. I help by guiding them to solutions to problems when they are troubled. I am here as a resource when they need me. When I am not physically available, I leave a phone number so I can be reached if there is an emergency. I am almost always available to them. But, in God's case it is not a matter of almost but always. He is continually available. The communication line to God never closes.

## Gloria's Comments

*As I read Bob's optimistic notes concerning his plans for the girls, I felt burdened with an irrepressible sadness over memories of the events that followed his divorce. Bob had been grievously hurt. He had consented to weekend visitation as part of the divorce decree and expected to maintain a fatherly role in his children's lives. He thought his ex-wife had married a responsible person. Instead, this man immediately set upon a path to discredit Bob, both to her and the children. He succeeded.*

*What started out as an amiable divorce became a horror story. Bob and I were put under a microscope. He picked at every minor incident that happened at our home and twisted it into something unpleasant to criticize us. We were hauled into court on erroneous charges. The children were barraged with propaganda to encourage the feeling that Bob did not love them.*

*After Bob's divorce, his older daughter Valerie, who was only eight years old, was enlisted to report back to her stepfather about every negative detail in our home. This must have caused her severe discomfort, because we had developed a warm relationship, and I knew that she really enjoyed her visits. She and my younger daughter Cindy, who was then twelve, were compatible playmates who entertained us with their performances and games each weekend.*

*What we did not realize was that Valerie's home life was dominated by a vicious, evil man who sought to keep her in sexual bondage, a man who appeared to be a saint to his wife. This person was highly regarded in his* community and was elected to the rank of elder in his church. He was glib, handsome and owned a successful business. He fooled everyone.

Valerie was old enough to see her mother's adoration for her new husband. She was aware of his prestige within their community. How confused she must have been by his assaults when he was held in such high regard in her world. How cunning he must have been at first to secure her loyalty before he set out to destroy her innocence. It was impossible for us to know all the violations of decent and moral conduct that existed in her home.

This villain, who later was indicted for three counts of rape and three counts of sodomy, and then comfortably plea bargained his way out of a just punishment for his crimes, was almost completely successful in disrupting the lives of Bob's children, their maternal relatives and our own immediate family. But for the grace of God, Bob would never have seen his children again. If God had not lifted His mighty hand against the Satanic assault directed at our family, we would have all been left deprived of the joyful reunion and personal growth that we have all now experienced.

The vast sorrow that I feel is heightened by the events that took place on Feb. 18, 1986. That was the day my husband handed over full authority of his children's lives to the obviously antagonistic, but seemingly capable hands, of their stepfather. That was the day he signed adoption papers that legally relinquished his fatherhood.

Prior to the time he signed those documents, the children's behavior had fully convinced Bob that they resented him being a part of their lives. They were fully allied with their stepfather in their refusal to see him. We were presented with evidence from psychologists that the children were emotionally disturbed at the thought of visitation, or any contact whatsoever, with their father. Our last court battle resulted in Bob's right to see his children at their church for only one hour a week, under the supervision of a pastor. Valerie was about fourteen years old at that time. She was adamant in her refusal to come to those meetings.

The last Christmas that Bob met with his children at the church he joyfully brought Santa along, fully garbed in his red suit, with all the presents in a large sack to be given to Regina and Patrick. The following week Regina reported that all his Christmas gifts were given away because they did not need anything from him, an obvious re-statement of what she had heard at home. Patrick, who was only five years old, responded to Bob's hugs by kicking him. Bob had tenaciously continued to meet with his two younger children at the church for another year or so, but gave up after he recognized he could not cope with the ongoing psychological bruising he received each time they met.

We then sought out the advise of a psychiatrist who recommended that he step out of his children's lives completely. He told us that the children were under extreme stress and that he was doing them harm by insisting that they see him. Bob bitterly complied by allowing the petition of adoption to go through. He hoped that what the psychiatrist said was valid; that his children would seek to know the truth when they were older, and that they would contact him later on. He allowed the adoption because he was convinced that all his court petitions for visitation would be denied due to the unbalanced emotional state of his children. He had reached a dead end in his attempts to be a good father.

Two years later, in 1988, Valerie courageously revealed the truth of her circumstance to the police. She was trying to protect her younger sister whose behavior problems she suspected were linked to the same abuse she herself had experienced. Threatened with the death of their mother, both girls had maintained resolute silence, not only from the world at large, but even from each other.

At last we understood that the campaign to separate Bob from his children was related to the cover-up of the abuse existing in the home. Amazingly, even after the villain's arrest, and the domestic separation that ensued, neither the children nor his ex-wife tried to contact Bob. Satan's bond on their lives continued even after the perpetrator of the crimes was no longer physically present.

It would be a while before we found out that their minds were still incapable of conceiving the thought that Bob would be even remotely interested in them. Their psyches had been so damaged that they fully believed that Bob was unconcerned with their welfare. Bob must have felt horrific pain when he first learned the truth about what had happened to his children.

Regina's letter was the beginning of the answer to his feeble and uncertain prayer asking for a reunion and re-bonding with his children. God was answering Bob's need even before he personally acknowledged Him.

# Chapter 6

## An Angel in Baltimore

Bob's journal continued
September, 10, 1990

I am convinced that no prayer is too small for God to answer, no everyday problem too insignificant to be addressed to the Lord. I now have belief that my prayers can be answered immediately if there is a need. For example, we were driving back from Canada with my parents and couldn't find a motel room that was afford-able. I was so exhausted that I knew it was dangerous for me to keep driving. I could have asked Gloria to take over, but I knew how prejudiced my father was against women drivers, so I let my machismo get in the way. I was even more reluctant to ask my seventy-three year old dad to take the wheel because I knew he was proba-bly just as tired as I was. I turned my thoughts to the Lord and asked him to help me stay awake. It was a small and simple prayer but I thought I'd give it a shot. Within the next five minutes, all my vitality returned and I was wide awake. That prayer was equivalent to ten cups of coffee.

By answering this prayer, God taught me that He could answer immediately if there was a need. This small request of mine was barely more than a thought, but it was answered anyway. God knows my needs, both great and small; but I know that now He wants me to come to Him in prayer so I will recognize that He is in charge of my life.

Another very significant answer to prayer took place at our last antique show. Since we gave up our antique shop, our entire income is dependent upon our sales at shows. Our needs were particularly great at the last show because we had some hefty bills to pay for the purchase of merchandise. We had recently gone into debt, buying some items that would bring a good profit when they sold. Our shows had not been bringing in enough money to reinvest, and all our income had been used for living expenses. When a good buying opportunity came along, I went out on a limb and borrowed money for the purchase.

During the set up for our most recent antique show in Baltimore, I remembered that I'd prayed for a specific amount of money to satisfy debts once before. The amount at that time was $7,000.00. Although our sales met this amount, we were left short when we paid off our consignment obligations. This time my prayer was even more specific. I told the Lord that I needed $9,000.00, irrespective of consignments, to satisfy our debts and leave us enough money to live on until our next scheduled exhibit. I was praying for an exact amount of sale generated money. On the first day of the show we took in a total of $200.00. On Saturday our sales at one p.m. added another $400.00.

I really hate situations that leave me hanging on hopes until the last hours of a show. I was starting to feel anxious, so I asked the Lord to provide us with enough sales that day to at least cover our minimum expenses. At three thirty p.m. we had a sale to another dealer that added up to $4,750.00. That brought us up to a total of $5,350, an amount which comfortably covered the expenses of the show and the cost of the merchandise sold. By five p.m. on Sunday we had sales totaling another $2,625.00. We now had a total of $8,025. The show was to close at six o'clock.

At five-fifty p.m. I was approached by a dealer who wanted to buy one of my vases. He admitted that he didn't have the ready cash. Earlier in the show I admired a pair of bowls in his booth. We worked out a trade plus some cash on his part, a deal that gave me total gross sales of $9,025.00 for the show. My specific prayer for a needed amount had been answered almost to the penny.

The show was miraculous not just because we realized our money objective. It was one of the worst attended shows we had ever done. All the other dealers were dissatisfied with their sales. The promoters of the show lost money because of the poor attendance. They announced that they were canceling future plans for another show at that location. Everyone was upset, except us. It was one of our best shows in a long time.

Aside from this obvious answer to our financial need and the resultant spiritual reconfirmation of God's hand in my life, Gloria and I both shared a message from the Lord on that Saturday night of the show. I am leaving an entry on this page for Gloria to tell the story of Bobby. Although I still don't know when I will reveal my faith to her or fully understand why God has led me to write this diary, I know that someday God's purpose will be served through it. I'm pretty sure it will be a book, and if it is, the story about Bobby is very important. So Gloria, when you read this section sometime in the future, please describe what happened with Bobby as you remember it.

## Gloria's Comments

*Before I write about our adventure with Bobby, I have to disclose my state of mind during the days preceding the Baltimore antique show that led to our acquaintance. The argument I had with Bob over Regina's mental illness was still fresh in my thoughts. Indeed, it had dominated all of our communication during the five hour trip to the show; and it still had not been resolved four days later.*

*We had stopped to visit Regina at Four Winds, a private mental hospital in upstate New York. Bob's ex-wife Ann had secured a job that provided insurance coverage for her daughter's private hospitalization. Regina was delighted to leave the state run Sagamore Children's facility. Four Winds was located in a rural area and was less institutional than what she'd experienced for the last two years. She was also allowed much more freedom. We were happily surprised that the doctors were allowing us to take her to a restaurant for dinner.*

*This was our first authorized visit with her outside an institution. We'd been granted very limited visitation with her in the past, only one hour once a week and always with a therapist present. We had not been allowed any visits at all for long periods of time . We would not have had much intimate contact with her if she hadn't been so resourceful at running away during hospitalizations. Her nickname of "happy feet" had been well earned. She was as ready as a young colt to spring out of the first open gate when she was feeling well.*

*Now, at last, we were together in a social setting, our first authorized visitation alone, with the full approval of the authorities in charge of her care. Bob was elated, thinking that our dinner was a taste of a future that promised the healing of her problems, a future that would be filled with the same relaxed atmosphere that we experienced then.*

*We thought we had a fairly accurate picture of Regina's problems. We knew that the results of her home life had left her emotionally unstable and that she had been examined by many psychiatrists who agreed that she was clinically depressed. We knew she had behavior problems that fell into a diagnosis of "borderline personality disorder," a condition that was treatable with psychotherapy. We were aware that her depression was being treated with effective medications. We had knowledge that she had used illegal drugs in the past as an escape, but we had hopes that she would voluntarily abandon them after her release from hospitalization. We were unprepared however, for what she told us at dinner.*

*As we talked, Regina told us about several prior hospitalizations that were unknown to us, indicating that she had many confinements before her stay at Sagamore Children's Hospital, the place from which she'd first contacted us. She discussed a recent diagnosis of schizo-affective disorder and manic depression, revealing information about hallucinations and "voices" that she was currently having. She spoke easily about these experiences thinking that we already knew the facts when, in reality, they were never shared with us until that very moment. As she dispassionately spoke about her problems, I was becoming more and more agitated.*

*I realized we were facing severe mental illness. Regina would be dependent upon a lifetime of medications which would require constant supervision. But it wasn't until she pulled up her sleeves to reveal recent scars of self mutilation, and told us that she had been having memory blackouts, that I realized I no longer wished to undertake full responsibility for her.*

*Bob had been promising Regina that he would take her home with us permanently after her hospital release. He planned to pay her as our assistant at antique shows so that he could keep an eye on her. Although I had some ambivalent feelings about taking this responsibility before, the new information about her condition left me trembling with apprehension and determined that I would not be willing to take on such a task. I both loved and pitied Regina; but I did not feel equipped to take on obligations that would fully commit me to her care. I did not feel capable of managing her illness.*

*When we brought Regina back to the hospital, I noticed that Bob was also shaken by the visit. Our resolves, however, were on totally opposite planes. He was convinced that Regina needed our help more than ever and that a loving family would help her to heal. I was appalled at the thought! We almost had an empty nest. Cheryl and Cindy were adults who would soon be moving out of our home, and I was looking forward to a one on one relationship with Bob, unfettered by attending to the needs of children. Most pointedly, this was not an ordinary child.*

*Not to my credit, I was also quite upset by the deep emotional response Bob was showing towards Regina and his other two children. Bob had resolutely attempted to conceal any deep emotions from me. It was part of his masculine posture, a heritage that was passed on from his father.*

*Now that his children reappeared in our lives, he revealed very observable tender emotion towards them. Cindy had recently commented to me that she felt hurt by his outward affection towards his children since he had never shown such closeness in his relationship with her. "I guess he never loved us the way I thought he did," she said.*

*I had never begrudged Bob any pleasure at his reunion with his kids, but I too was shocked by the amount of expressive love he was able to give them. Bob showed a sensitivity that I had never seen before. I had been witness to his selfless love since Regina entered our lives again and I was hurt because he had concealed this side of himself from me. I felt left out. I had no idea that his increased sympathy might be related to his now well-established faith in the Lord. So, when Bob said that Regina would come home to live with us, I responded with a loud and definite no! We argued.*

*Our conflict over the problems (provoked by our Wednesday visit with Regina) persisted until Saturday night when we met Bobby. I will never forget him.*

*There he was, sitting across from us at the table, a shabby man in his late forties, whose presence made me feel uncomfortable. I'd first noticed him as he walked towards us through the Baltimore Inner Harbor Mall. I was seated in the food court, just watching people pass by as I waited for Bob to return with a platter of shrimp. As Bob brought the food over, the man stopped walking and watched us. He pointed at the dish of shrimp and then to himself, asking in gesture if he could share our meal. Before I could react negatively to the idea, Bob beckoned him with a come-on-over gesture of his own. Bob and I had not exchanged one word before the man quickly seated himself across from us. I had alarms going off in my head.*

*Even before Bob pantomimed his welcome, I had known that there was something odd about this stranger. His clothing and expression were noticeably unconventional. I immediately recognized that he was mentally ill. He had a countenance that Regina sometimes had, one of being only partially involved with externals and of being inner focused. I felt near to panic. I was in no mood to deal with more mental illness.*

*Across the table sat Bobby, happily devouring our "peel your own" shrimp, his soiled hands sharing from the same bowl of food that we were eating. I felt the same revulsion I'd experienced when I saw the reddened scars on Regina's wrists.*

*"Why," I thought, "do I have to endure this? Bob and*

*I are hardly speaking to each other. The show is not going well. Is he inviting this character to our table just to annoy me? I don't want to eat anything from this dish. I wish I could just go back to the hotel, to my clean room, to the safety of my privacy."*

*At Bob's prompting, Bobby began to tell his life story as it evolved from the diagnosis of schizophrenia at age seventeen through the thirty years he spent in a mental hospitals. For the past two years he had been living independently in a furnished room and working as a volunteer doing clean up chores at a local store. He revealed his pride at finally being able to survive outside an institution. He recounted his struggles to find a niche in a world that is intolerant of mental illness.*

*As he spoke, my initial revulsion was replaced by sympathy and I found myself carelessly picking from the diminished bowl of shrimp in front of me, now unconcerned with the sanitary conditions that had bothered me only short minutes before. I sat with tear filled eyes, reacting to the tragedy of a life spent in mental hospitals. Sadly, I realized that Bobby's past was an account of Regina's future if her condition did not improve.*

*I felt the pain of his loneliness. I listened as Bobby spoke about his only sexual experience with another patient, which he said was begun with respect and dignity after she granted her full permission for the intimacy. He went on to say that he was a "good boy" who never fought except for the one time he defended a patient who was being mistreated by a hospital attendant. How like Regina he was! How willing to risk the punishment of the institution in order to aid a helpless patient.*

*He spoke of his regret at never having the opportunity for a normal relationship with his mother and father because they were also institutionalized with schizophrenia at an early age. We learned that he was raised by his older brother until he reached the age of seventeen and his first hospitalization began.*

*Bobby remembered starting life as a normal child. As he progressed into adolescence he gradually felt reality slipping away. He began to hear voices and started to hallucinate. He realized he was developing the same condition he'd observed in his parents when he was younger, but he was powerless to stop the progress of his illness.*

*Seated before me was a boy-man, now proud that he was out in society, committed to helping others through his voluntary work, but still crying out for the loving childhood he had never known. Repeatedly, he said, "I was a good boy; I never did anything bad." Repeatedly he looked straight at Bob and said, "If I could have, I would have wanted for you to be my daddy. Would you be my daddy if you could have been?" Over and over Bob replied, "Yes, I would."*

*Bobby did not ask me if I would have liked to be his mother. When he did turn to me he was talking about angels. He said that everyone has a guardian angel. Then he said something that startled me. Looking at me and then turning to Bob he said, "She is your guardian angel."*

*Tears are falling, my heart is aching as I remember how far I was from reflecting God's light to my husband at that time. Angel indeed! I was his enemy. I was trying* to stop him from helping his child.

After we said goodbye to Bobby, Bob and I walked back to the hotel in complete silence, our arms locked together in mutual need for comfort, both of us trying to dispel the depression that enveloped us.

It was not until we entered the hotel and stood at the elevator that our silence was broken. As we faced each other I noticed that Bob's eyes were as reddened as mine. His overflowed with pity, mine were filled with remorse. The significance of the experience was just beginning to form in my mind. I said to Bob, "God is trying to tell me something very important."

By the time the key was in the lock, I had the revelation that we had just met an angel. Two steps into the room and I knew that God had bestowed an almost unbelievable blessing upon me personally. He had sent us a Messenger and the message was that Bob was to press forward with his plan to take Regina home. But, more importantly, the message that I received that night was to support Bob in every earthly and spiritual way and to guide him towards his goal. I had been elected to oversee his efforts and protect them. God had seen fit to intervene and show me the way. He had mercifully sent us an angel in the form of a schizophrenic man named Bobby to set me straight.

Earlier in his journal, Bob had questioned whether or not supposed messages from God could otherwise be explained as chance or coincidence. This experience was not a coincidence. It was a God-incidence of wondrous proportions.

The Lord's intent was clear. We had just become aware of the severity of Regina's diagnosis. It had caused *division between us. He then sent us to meet a schizophrenic man who exhibited an illness that was just as disturbing as Regina's problems. We were both united in sympathy towards him. This stranger requested that Bob take a stand on parenting and I was told to act as a guardian of Bob's efforts.*

*Meeting an angel is a humbling experience. I was completely overwhelmed by Jesus' love at the moment I recognized God's purpose. Warmth flooded through my body as if I could almost palpably feel His touch. The Lord's message was a gentle rebuke, given with so much love that I accepted it on the spot. I was now fully convinced that God intended Regina to come home to us and that I was going to help it happen. God opened my stubborn heart to His will, and I immediately responded with the obedient "yes" that my husband sought from me four days earlier. God required that we be unified in purpose in order to fulfill His plan. He sent His Messenger to soften my heart and clarify my role in Bob's endeavors.*

*Two days later, I related the amazing events to my sister-in-law Carol. She told me we had met an "angel unaware." It was the first time I'd heard the term. I recognized how appropriate it was in this circumstance.*

Bob's journal continued
February, 1991

It's been three months since my last entry in this journal. A lot has happened including Regina's rehospitalization in a Louisiana mental hospital, where she was sent after her stay at Four Winds. Gloria and I are down in Florida doing a series of antique shows. Regina called just before we left, asking if I would attend a week long family counseling session in Louisiana along with her mother and brother Patrick. The hospital encounter is required before her graduation into life outside an institution. I really felt guilty about leaving Gloria alone to set up the show by herself. She encouraged me to go despite her own feelings of discomfort. I'm sure she wasn't happy at the thought of me spending a week with my former wife and children as part of a family-oriented group. But, since this all has to do with Regina's welfare, she had a positive attitude.

I rented a car which I shared with Ann and Patrick as we drove back and forth from the hospital. We were staying at the same motel which pleased my son greatly because he could negotiate between both rooms. He had his mom and dad under the same roof for the first time he could remember. Although I had anticipated our family relationship to be strained, we wound up having breakfast and dinners together. Ann was pleasant, and our mutual goal of restoring Regina to health added to the cordiality.

The counseling sessions included several other families whose relatives were also getting ready to leave the hospital. Regina, my little angel, was the star of the show. Everyone, doctors and nurses, aides and patients, gave us glowing reports of her progress. Her delight at seeing us together as a family again, without any evidence of hostility, was glowingly evident. Our older daughter Valerie, already a mother at age twenty, was living in Western Canada at the time. She was not expected to attend.

The hospital focused on problem sharing among the families, and the hospital staff lectured us on dysfunctional families. It certainly was an eye opener for me. I did not relate to the dysfunction of my former family, because the tragedy responsible for damaging my children concerned their relationship with Ann's new husband. I did get zapped, however, in regard to my present marriage, and how I had behaved in relation to my wife and stepdaughters.

When I got back to Florida to rejoin Gloria at the show, I was anxious to apologize for some of my behavior during our marriage. I realized that I'd targeted Gloria for all the blame regarding the discipline and behavior of her children. She had become the scapegoat for everything that had gone wrong in the family. Her children blamed her for giving so much of her energy and time to me (exactly the way I wanted it), and for not being a larger part of their daily lives. I recognized my selfishness. I had been replaying my own father's role of being a husband who insisted upon respect and discipline while ignoring the emotional needs of his wife and family. The "sins of the father" were being carried on through me.

Gloria was astounded at my insight and accepted my apology, but only after getting in some digs about incidents which further convicted me. It was fun to watch her get a charge out of putting me in my place, because she was having such a good time doing it in a playful way.

It may have been the psychiatrists who informed me about my behavior, but it surely was God that lead me to apologize. I think my dad's macho behavior, which I'd internalized, would have prevented any overt repentance in the years before I had my personal relationship with the Lord. I imagine I have behaved this way in my former marriage too, although my memories are hazy. I suppose I gave Ann good reason to want a divorce. Gloria, however, is totally committed to me no matter what I've done that has been unfair. For this, I love her all the more!

## Gloria's comments

*Instead of Regina coming home to us within the next month as predicted, she regressed soon after the meeting. The hospital thought it best to delay her release despite her protests. She was still a minor and had little choice in the matter. Her "happy feet" carried her out into the surrounding community several times, but she was apprehended quickly. Once she reported that it had taken six attendants to finally corner her and take her in. She enjoyed all the attention that her escapes engendered.*

*It would not be until June, five months later, that she would be released. At age eighteen she had the legal right to make her own decisions. Regina would defy her doctor's recommendation in her efforts to reach the safety of her father's house. She wanted to be part of a normal family, just as Bobby did. She wanted her daddy.*

# Chapter 7

## Tomorrow, Tomorrow, I Love You Tomorrow

Bob's journal continued
March 26, 1991

Life with the Lord certainly is an exciting adventure. I am discovering, from both my reading and experience, that the Holy Spirit has really been moving me in the right direction without my realization of the work He is doing in my life. While Jesus acts as my intercessor in bringing my petitions to the Father, the Holy Spirit enables things to happen. I now recognize that the inner voice I hear is His. I was never aware that He is so personal and instructive.

This is not to say that I didn't have a conscience before I had His Presence. I wrote early on in the journal that since childhood I always had a strong sense of right and wrong. My morality, however, was primarily shaped by my home life and teachers at school. If my childhood had been other than it was, I might not have had this sense of accountability. It occurs to me that our free will is influenced by the value systems that are internalized in our early childhood. Our early experiences become part of our subconscious and we later act on them as if by instinct. Some of our decisions as adults are unconsciously prompted by our early sense of right and wrong. As adults we may perform some very antisocial acts, without any awareness or concern for how they effect others. If God's morality isn't a part of our early conditioning, it is likely that our own personal morality will be out of accord with His.

One thing I've noticed about the indwelling Holy Spirit is that He has a mind of His own. Many times He guides me against my own personal sense of what is right and appropriate. He does this by giving me a jab of conscience. Many times, this jab is directly opposed to my conscious awareness of what is acceptable and I know that this jolt of disapproval comes from Him. I then have a choice of acting on my own will or listening to the direction of my Teacher.

If the Lord had not seen fit to send us the Holy Spirit as a personal Helper, Christianity would not have become the vital force that it is today. God would still be worshipped but each person would still be acting out his own early conditioned concept of right and wrong.

The Holy Spirit helps us to modify our will to His will. I've learned that this is not a one-time experience. Wouldn't it be wonderful if our rebirth through faith in Jesus brought an immediate change that would put us in perfect accord with God's will for our lives? But, it's not so. The Holy Spirit comes to us just as we are when we confess Jesus as our Lord and Savior. Then, as an indwelling personality, He instructs us, guides us, comforts us and leads us to the place He wants us to be. This can only happen over time. As we deal with life situations, the Spirit encourages us to modify our way of thinking and to reform the unconscious value system that we brought with us when we first gave our lives to Christ. The Holy Spirit is the Enabler who can lift us above our own flawed temperaments and bring us closer to Christ. He leads us to a new understanding of ourselves and others.

As a Christian, for I now know that I am, I am part of a great supernatural adventure. I'm no longer acting on my sole will. I have another Person inside me who can actually act to refine my thoughts and actions by revealing new truths to me. I'm amazed at His Presence. I now look forward to each tomorrow to see what new situation the Lord places me in as His student.

Gloria recently told me that she notices that I have much more patience than I've shown in the past. If so, this is a perfect example of the works of the Spirit in my life. I can think of two incidences that happened recently that reflect this.

We were waiting in line at the gas station. There was only one person in line in front of me. I was in a hurry. It was taking the fellow in front of us a long time to fill his tank. In my impatience, my instinct was to spin out around him to the empty pump in front. If I had, I would have smacked into another car which was passing on the right in my "blind spot." Gloria could have been hurt. Two, perhaps three cars, would have been involved in an unnecessary accident that was provoked by my impatience.

The second incident occurred when I was at the check out counter of a supermarket. An elderly lady stood in front of me, fumbling with her money. I thought she was taking too much time. It was annoying for me to stand there when I had so many other things to do. I was tempted to help her to find the correct amount to pay her bill. If I had interfered by helping the transaction to go quickly, I would have made the woman feel that she was incapable of handling her affairs, a feeling she probably was facing daily, as was apparent by her frailty and advanced age. I would have succeeded in getting out of the supermarket earlier, but it would have cost this women some of her dignity. Instead of acting impatiently, the Holy Spirit had me take a deep breath and smile.

In both these cases the Holy Spirit was acting as a protector. In the first instance, He protected us and others from physical harm. In the second, He stopped me from hurting the feelings of another human being and protected me from having the inevitable guilt I would have felt. The old lady did not walk away insulted. There was a "fringe benefit" transferred over to her as a result of my acting in God's Spirit. In a greater sense it would seem that the behavior of Christians, acting in the will of the Holy Spirit, has a kind of spill-over effect that can benefit others who may not even be aware of it. All the little old lady saw was a kind gentleman who was smiling at her. How different her day would have been if I'd intruded by counting out her change for her.

I guess I am answering the Spirit today by making this entry in my journal. If I don't record these events, I probably will forget them easily. They are just two small incidents in my life, but they become important when they highlight the work of the Holy Spirit. Since I have extended my formal prayer life by simply talking to God as things come up during my day, there have been many evidences of His response and I'm certain that I wouldn't remember them if I hadn't written them down.

2 p.m.

Bingo! A few minutes ago we received a letter from the attorney announcing that the patent office is going to allow our patent to go through with a few minor changes. It will take several months. I think the drawings need some modification. Our lawyer can't believe that our "dumb" idea is going to be patented. Anyway, it's now time to get started approaching companies. I feel strongly that I should submit the idea to Phillip Morris. Gloria feels that a tobacco company would not be interested in a non-smoking devise. My interest is sparked by a recent newspaper article that announced their purchase of a candy company overseas. But, in this case, I'm not at all sure that it is God's direction or my own. I'm going to send out the information. Time will tell.

March 29, 1991

Gloria's mother, who has been in a nursing home, has decided to come and live with us. This means we will have to add an extension to the house. Large extension or small, that is the question. I told Gloria I would decide within a day. After praying, I received another message from the Lord. He said that he had already told me to plan on our daughters' singing group. He said Valerie was going to move from Canada and be living with us . I've decided to put on a large extension.

I hadn't heard the Spirit's voice in several months. Maybe I just stopped listening! I casually told Gloria that I believe Valerie is going to be living with us. "With or without her husband?", she asked. I didn't really know how to answer. The message just said Valerie. Anyway, Gloria did not respond favorably to the idea.

With Cheryl and Cindy still living at home and Regina due to move in soon, the last thing she wants is more kids. Valerie would come with her two little ones. I'm sure if Gloria knew that this prophecy was from the Lord, she would have accepted it differently. Right now she thinks I'm losing my mind.

Lord, you have such a good sense of humor. Send some of it to Gloria, please!

## Gloria's Comments

*Bob had always been such an optimist. His good humor in looking forward to every day did not represent any big changes in his personality at this time. As a matter of fact, I thought all his ideas were self-motivated, and I felt quite left out of his plans. I would never have guessed that his confidence about Nic Stics, Regina's recovery, and Valerie coming here to live, was based on knowledge given to him by the Holy Spirit. I didn't think he knew the Lord in any personal way.*

*If Bob thought I had no sense of humor at that time, it*

*was because I was too busy trying to juggle bills, take care of the house and help my children resolve problems which they felt were insurmountable. I was also responsible for planning our antique shows. My greatest commitment, however, involved writing (with a deadline) a resource book on Oriental antiques.*

*While Bob was having a good time with the Lord, I was praying for the strength to take care of all my obligations. I'd started to resent his cheerfulness, the very quality that had attracted me to him in the first place. There just didn't seem to be that much to be happy about. I didn't want any increased burdens. I felt overwhelmed.*

Bob's journal continued
April 4, 1991

We were seated at our kitchen table today when Gloria said, "I have an idea." She says this at least twice a day. Her ideas are usually a free associated thinking out loud. My thoughts were, "Oh, no, not again!" because as a rule her ideas don't seem significant to me and I tell her to forget them. This time, however, I had an instantaneous message from the Lord that said, "Listen to her now and pay close attention." I was amazed, as usual, to be so strongly directed by the Spirit.

Gloria said she thought that it would be a good idea to use some of the profits we get from Nic Stics to put together a newsletter with individuals' personal accounts of answered prayer.

I almost fell off the chair with surprise. If she had substituted the word *book* for newsletter, I think I really would have tipped the chair in my excitement. I knew that she was going to say something special, because God had already told me to pay attention, and I had never paid much attention to her casual comments before.

The idea she presented was far afield of our usual conversations, which were generally concerned with antiques, our children, or the possible success of our invention. Her idea should have referred to any of these things because she knows nothing about the journal, nothing about my prayer life, nothing about our potential book.

I'd received a message from the Spirit telling me not to let her know anything about my plans for the profits derived from Nic Stics until we received some advance royalty on the product. I was also told not to mention anything about God's involvement to anyone else until the book comes out.

Sometimes this whole experience seems unreal to me because I haven't been allowed to share it with others. I think that the Holy Spirit gave Gloria a message for me, which would reaffirm my relationship to Him and make His plan for my life clearer. I'd better pay closer attention to what she says in the future.

April 11, 1991

I'm starting to feel afraid that I am really going to be elected to spread God's word. I feel very inadequate. Can I hold up? Can I do all this right? I'm excited and fearful at the same time. Why did He choose me? I hardly understand the Bible when I try to read it. I don't even go to church. How could He ever have picked me?

April 25, 1991

We were sitting down for dinner yesterday with three of our children: Valerie, who is visiting from Canada, Patrick and Cindy. Suddenly, I was aware of that unmistakable inner voice directing that grace be said before our meal.

The only time we say grace at a meal is when we visit my brother's house, or when he comes here for dinner. My typical response to being asked to give thanks before a meal would be, "Grace, let's eat." Gloria has never said grace before a meal either. Yet, within a few seconds of the Spirit's message, Gloria said, "Bob, don't you want to say grace?"

Again, I asked myself, "Where did this idea come from?" Is she reading my mind or is she picking up on the messages that the Spirit is sending to me? Is the Spirit using her once again to confirm the validity of my relationship to Him? Unaccustomed as I am to public praying, and not wanting to appear out of character, I passed the request back to her.

## Gloria's comments

*Obviously, Bob was still acting out his conditioned role of male chauvinist at the time of these journal entries. Not interested in my ideas! I am not a mind reader. If I was picking up "vibes" having to do with his thoughts and projects, it was because the Holy Spirit was active in my life as well. Most likely, the Spirit was showing Bob that my input was important and that he should value my opinions more than he did. Even though Bob respected my intelligence as an individual, he still retained some very old world views about our roles as a couple. The Bible tells us that Eve was created as a helper for Adam. "Helper" is one of the names that Jesus used to designate the Holy Spirit in the New Testament. Wives are supposed to minister to their husbands as Christ ministered his to His disciples. Within scant days of Jesus facing his destiny on the cross, He knelt and washed the feet of His disciples at the Passover meal. In a figurative sense, I had been washing Bob's feet since we were married. I was following Paul's directive to be submissive to my husband but was Bob loving me as God loves the Church?*

"Husbands, love your wives, just as Christ also loved the church and gave Himself up for her;" (Ephesians 5:25)
"So husbands ought also to love their own wives as their own bodies. He who loves his own wife loves himself;
for no one ever hated his own flesh, but nourishes and cherishes it, just as Christ also does the church." (Ephesians 5:28-29)

*By not respecting the value of my ideas and opinions in the past, Bob had diminished my role as his partner. It is a comfort for me to know that the Holy Spirit was acting to change Bob's attitude towards me at that time.*

*I was truly dismayed with the responsibilities I had to face daily. I was too busy to feel depressed, which would have been my typical reaction to facing burdensome tasks. The word "frenzy" best typifies my life at the time of Bob's last journal entry. I was totally respon-*

sible for all the writing necessary to produce our book on Oriental antiques. I had to do extensive research. I had neither the time or privacy to do either.

Every bedroom in our four bedroom home was dedicated to a resident or visiting child. Valerie and her baby had visited us several times, usually staying six weeks, anxious to participate in the family life she was deprived of in her upbringing. We were all happy that she came, but it certainly interfered with my writing time.

Cindy was depressed and needed time to talk. She had been traveling between our home and California where she was attempting to launch a career as a make-up artist. Most of the time she was home and out of work. Cheryl, my older daughter, was trying to readjust her life and she also needed my emotional support. I was in charge of the family and business checkbooks, both of which were frequently empty. I became an expert juggler of bills during this period. I anticipated Regina's arrival from the hospital in Louisiana sometime soon, and I had concerns about her future with us. I had the usual household chores to contend with; frequently ignoring them with a lingering sense of guilt.

I was also preoccupied with Bob's behavior which seemed unrealistic to me when I related it to the stress on our lives. True that he smoked more than ever, at least three packs a day, yet he seemed totally unconcerned about our hectic household and the problems that I faced daily. I was becoming resentful of his calm attitude and I felt that I handled all our problems by myself.

Yet, Bob was being changed in more ways than we both realized. Regina would be arriving soon, and her homecoming was going to modify Bob's life in both the way he related to me and to himself. Her residence would set off a series of circumstances that would create changes in his emotional and physical being. Ultimately, God would use Regina to change our whole family by presenting us with a series of interventions that could not be termed anything but miraculous.

# Chapter 8

## An Attack of the Heart

Bob's journal continued
July 21, 1991

I haven't written in this journal for quite a while. So much has happened. While at a show in Cleveland, Ohio at the end of May, I received a message from Regina via our answering machine, telling us that she was about to be discharged from the hospital, and requesting that we come down to Louisiana immediately to pick her up. Another of my prayers was about to be answered.

We arrived on Tuesday evening just in time to visit with Regina at the hospital. She was so excited. Her first words to us were, "I'm all packed." After we caught up on the latest family news, Regina told us that we would meet with her psychiatrist the next day to arrange her discharge.

When we met with the doctor, I was surprised at the

tone of the meeting. We had anticipated that he felt that she was ready to go home. Instead, he informed us that Regina was being released at her own request. She had reached her eighteenth birthday and could not be held there against her will. He explained that she'd had several set backs since I'd visited for the family conference, and that he was not sure she was ready to live with her family. He had advised her to move to a nearby halfway house and continue with her therapy at the hospital instead.

He told us about the heavy medications she was taking, one of which had to be monitored by a laboratory once a week. He stated that she would have to contact a psychiatrist immediately if she went home with us, emphasizing that we were to anticipate that she would have some future hospitalizations. He suggested that we take her out of the hospital for the next two days and see what developed. If everything worked out and Regina still wanted to go, he would then reluctantly sign the discharge on Friday.

When Gloria and I went back to our hotel room, she revealed her fears to me. I was also feeling uneasy, but I wanted Regina with me badly enough to take whatever risk was necessary. I told Gloria that we would take the doctor's advise and just wait to see what developed over the next two days.

We spent both days sightseeing with Regina. She seemed fine to me. Gloria also relaxed enough to agree that Regina would come home with us. We started out for home on Friday, equipped with a list of instructions concerning Regina's medications, a referral to a psychiatrist, and an invitation for Regina to return to the hospital if she felt her condition was deteriorating. It was to be her first time away from a hospital setting in almost four years. I was as happy as a new father who was bringing home his first baby. I felt like handing out cigars. Regina was going to be okay. I would make sure of it.

As I had planned, we took Regina with us as a paid assistant to our next antique show on the first weekend of June. She seemed to be doing very well. She befriended some of the staff and even went out to tour the town with one of the men who provided us with showcases. She spent most of the show chatting with the guys at the coffee concession. She managed to talk them into supplying free cups of gourmet coffee for all of us during the weekend. I thought she was doing just fine.

On Monday of the next week, I took her shopping for a new outfit to wear to the show we were going to do that Saturday and Sunday. Suddenly, during our walk through the shopping mall, Regina said that we had to leave immediately. By the time we got to the car she was talking to herself, responding to her inner voices. She started screaming, cursing and pounding the dashboard. I tried and tried to break through to her. She finally acknowledged with a nod of head that she could hear me. Soon after she was sobbing in my arms. The crisis was over, but not for me.

As soon as we got home and I was alone with Gloria, I started to tell her what happened and I broke down myself. I couldn't contain my grief over the pain my child was suffering. Regina's illness suddenly became real to me. I hadn't wanted to see it. For the first time, I was really concerned about her chances of living a normal life. My heart was breaking.

By the time the weekend came and we all went to the show, I found myself watching Regina very closely. She seemed very composed since she'd had a medication adjustment earlier in the week. It was not until three days later, on Wednesday, June 12th, that there was another crisis. It wasn't Regina this time. It was me. My heart was not just emotionally breaking, it was breaking in fact.

I recognized what was happening to me mostly because of my medical corps training in the Navy. There was a slight nausea, perspiration, and the telltale pain down my left arm. During the drive to the hospital, Gloria and I both knew I was having a heart attack. Neither of us mentioned those words because it would have made it too real, and we didn't want to panic. Surprisingly, the electrocardiogram didn't show any unusual activity, but the doctor told us he would like me to stay the night for observation.

The doctor left us alone as they wheeled the machinery out of the emergency room. Gloria looked nervous. To reassure her, I sat up laughing as I reached out to grab her arm. My smile froze abruptly. At that instant I felt as if a large elephant had just landed on my chest. Gloria watched me fall back on the hospital gurney. Instinctively knowing what to do, she ran down the hall and brought the doctor back yelling for the technicians to return with the electrocardiogram machinery. As five or six interns stood around, the doctor told them how lucky they were to be witnessing a heart attack in progress on the EKG machine.

I was then rushed into the cardiac emergency room and administered Streptocanaise to stop the attack from progressing. Two hours later, I was still in pain. The emergency room people apparently didn't notice, but Gloria did by way of a small chink in the door. They would not let her in to see me. Rules don't stop Gloria when she has a mission, and hers was to see me survive.

She came into the room, saw my condition, and marched over to the doctor in charge. She asked how long the medication should take to stop the attack. After being told that it works within two hours she strongly insisted that it had not worked within that time frame and that he'd just better take a closer look at me. Within five minutes I was given a dose of T.P.A. and felt an almost immediate release of pain. Gloria was right there at my side to protect me as my guardian angel, just as Bobby, our angel in Baltimore, had said.

Two weeks later, I had my first angioplasty, knowing that I would have to go back in a month for another. Gloria was holding down the fort at home, caring for Regina, canceling shows, and running back and forth to the hospital to see me. On the basis of my enzyme count, the doctors told her I had suffered a major heart attack and would not be able to go back to our work, since it required a lot of lifting and long hours of driving.

I told Gloria that they were nuts and that I was going to be fine. I kept laughing and joking with the doctors and nurses, even during the angioplasty procedure. I thought the doctor's prognosis was "off the wall," but Gloria insisted that I was the one who had lost touch with reality. "You're in denial," she kept saying.

I confess that I was really cruel to her. I insulted her in front of my brother and told her to get out of my room and go home. I didn't want to hear her anymore. I hated being in the hospital. I wanted to get home to Regina. I felt lost without my cigarettes and the hospital food was not to my liking. I was happy to be released ten days later.

Within two weeks I was back in the hospital again. The other angioplasty had to be done early because I was getting new pains down my arm. After this procedure, I was given an appointment for a thallium stress test and sent home with instructions to do a lot of walking, adjust my diet, and stop smoking. I had survived a ninety-nine percent blockage in two major arteries.

During the two weeks between procedures, Regina decided to go back to the hospital in Louisiana. She couldn't stand the pressure of my illness and blamed herself in spite of our reassurance that years of smoking, poor eating habits and some excess weight gain were responsible. She had started hearing her voices again and had cut her wrists superficially.

It is important to record that I was not the least bit worried about my survival during the heart attack or angioplasties. I knew that God had many plans for me and that He would protect me no matter what the doctors said. I was right. Although my enzyme counts were high, the stress test revealed that actual damage was confined to about eight percent of the lower part of my heart. It was hardly affecting the pumping action at all. I was going to be able to continue to work and carry on life as usual.

A visiting priest was offering communion on the day before my last procedure. He informed me that one person out of a thousand did not make it through an angioplasty. I guess he wanted to make sure that I was in a right situation with God. That night, I told Gloria that my odds were good in order to reassure her She retorted with, "Well, he's wrong. The odds are one in a hundred."What was she trying to do, force me to feel afraid?

## Gloria's comments

*As I read this part of Bob's journal, I relived my memories of that time. When Bob recognized his heart attack symptoms he was sitting comfortably on the sofa watching television, holding Regina's hand. We were totally unprepared. He'd never had angina pains or any other symptom of heart trouble. I called our HMO immediately for permission to get him to the hospital. They asked for the location of the nearest facility. Knowing that the closest hospital did not have a reputation for swift emergency care, I lied and reported the university hospital which was farther from our house. I was determined that Bob would get the best care possible. On the way, Bob smoked two cigarettes. There I was, driving nervously to the best hospital I knew, trying to save his life, and he sat there in the passenger seat trying to kill himself before we got there. I was furious and frightened at the same time. I remember my frustration at not being able to communicate my anger about his smoking, afraid that my comments could launch further symptoms.*

*On the morning after his attack, I went to the library and found as many books as I could find to educate myself on heart disease. I was full of questions and concerns. Would Bob be eligible for social security disability payments? How could I manage Regina's illness and still shield Bob from anxiety? Could we continue to have sexual relations?*

*I couldn't sleep well at night while he was recovering in the hospital so I pored over every book. When I went to see Bob each day, I spurted out information like a walking encyclopedia of heart attacks. He wasn't in the least bit interested. He was too busy kidding with the nurses, the same nurses who would approach me quietly outside his room to ask me if my husband realized that he really was a sick man. By the time Bob told me what the priest said about the odds of fatalities resulting from angioplasty procedures, I was armed and ready to correct him with the lower odds. I was totally fed up with the casual attitude he exhibited about his condition. I wanted to shock him into reality.*

*It didn't work. He just laughed at me for trying to make him worry.*

*While Bob was in the hospital cheerfully recovering, and I was trying to adjust to his illness and plan a new life style, Regina was busy with her own plans to get readmitted to the hospital in Louisiana. She called and told her doctor what had happened to her father, explaining that she felt suicidal. The doctor agreed to take her back provided that she promise to enter a halfway house when she was discharged. Regina left for Louisiana a few days after Bob returned home.*

*I was intensely relieved. The cardiologist had told me that he felt Bob's heart attack was a result of genetic factors and recent stress. Having Regina around was bound to be stressful. Of course, Bob, with his characteristic optimism, was already thinking of his next opportunity to take her home. In the meantime, he was preoccupied with going back to work and launching the Nic*

100

*Stics project.*

*As Bob carried on with his plans, I was insisting that he participate in my project to get him to stop smoking and take his health more seriously. I got us involved in psychological counseling, hoping that my feelings could be articulated better in the presence of an impartial third party. I said what I had to say for nine sessions before the counselor advised me that I'd better be prepared to make an adjustment in my own thinking. Bob was not about to be convinced that I was right. I know I felt more indignant than hurt at the end of this last session. Bob was obviously not going to take my concerns seriously.*

*I was going to have to adjust and I was seething with resentment. I suddenly hated my life. My feelings were worth absolutely nothing to my husband. Didn't he realize that I was trying to help him avoid another possibly fatal heart attack later on, or a possible stroke that would leave him a permanent invalid?*

*If Bob had only shared his faith with me at that time, I could have worked out my fears. I would never have doubted that God had given him a personal assurance of victory. I knew that He had the power to do so.*

*I had one resource that remained untapped. I could have turned to the Lord myself, but I was too bitter about Bob's carelessness and too exhausted to pray. My prayer life had gone flat. I was relying completely upon myself to make changes in Bob's attitude. I know now that my refusal to turn my problems over to God when I was in despair left a clear path for Satan to influence my subconscious thoughts and weaken my trust in my husband.*

*The Master Deceiver, the Liar of Liars, the Tempter,*

*moved in swiftly to influence my thinking. By not pray-
ing and deliberately shutting off the inner voice of the
Holy Spirit, I permitted a wall of resentment, depression,
self-pity and detachment to encircle me. It happened so
quietly, this entrapment, that I hardly noticed it take
place. I went on playing my role as dutiful wife. Bob did
not notice any change. I was still an active partner in all
our pastimes. I still felt that I loved Bob, but I just didn't
want to be emotionally rocked by his attitudes and
decisions anymore. My heart had also been attacked.*

*I still loved God, but I was keeping Him at a distance,
putting Him in the same place I'd put my husband; still
there but out of the path of my emotions. How ironic
that we can still have faith and be so disobedient and
that Satan can set out snares for us even though we have
been born again in Christ.*

# Chapter 9

## God and the New York Times

Bob's journal continued
September 12, 1991

I'm on the road again, back to a rigorous show schedule, and I feel great. I've been hiring porters to do all the heavy lifting for me, and Gloria has taken over some of our unpacking chores. I asked the Lord specifically for $8,000.00 at our first show but we ended up with only $6,200.00 by closing at six 6 p.m. on Sunday. At seven forty-five p.m. during pack out, a couple came in with special permission to buy several pieces they had asked me to put away earlier in the show. When they didn't show up before closing, I assumed the sale was dead and then sold one of the pieces to another dealer.

With one of the important pieces gone, the couple decided not to buy the rest. I would have made an another $1,600.00 sale. I heard the Holy Spirit say to me,

"Not enough faith." It was a happy voice I heard, sounding as if He had played a big joke on me.

It's getting to be fun hanging around with the Lord and discovering His sense of humor. We had two more shows to do in our circuit, one in Chicago and another in Baltimore. While talking to God during the drive I said, "Okay Lord, you really got me on that one, now all I ask is that we have two $8,000.00 dollar shows. I blew the last one by not believing You, but I promise to let You handle the next two shows.

Well, not only didn't we make a profit in Chicago, we actually ended up losing $1,600.00. Boy, was I surprised! Once again, I was talking to God informally while driving to Baltimore. "Lord, what do I really know about anything? All I know is that everything is up to you. Maybe I'm supposed to be in the hole for $1,600.00. Did I do something wrong?" Some seconds later I heard the Spirit's voice say to me, "Don't you ever learn?".

"Learn what?", I replied. "I thought we had a deal."

When we arrived in Baltimore, I was still hoping for the $8,000.00 that I had asked for. Boy, did the Lord have a surprise for me. We had sales of $18,000.00 at the show. It was incredible. We got our $8,000.00 doubled plus another $2,000.00 to cover our loses on the last show.

September 29, 1991

We just finished another show in Detroit and the Lord came through for us again. Most of the dealers didn't do well. Since I have already told the Lord that we need a minimum of about $8000.00 a show, I'm not going to ask anymore. I know He will take care of us.

While we were at the Detroit show we received a call from the Patent Editor of The New York Times. The patent is now approaching final issue and he read about it in an office release. He has interviewed Gloria by phone and he will review it in his weekly patent column in the New York Times. Our lawyer told us that inventors were always seeking this kind of free publicity, and he couldn't believe that the editor had chosen Nic Stics to review. This has never happened to one of his clients before.

What a conformation that Nic Sticks was really God's Idea.! This invention required no prototype, no engineering plans, no scientific background on my part. I had nothing more to do than present the idea that God gave me and He did all the rest.

The New York Times, Saturday, September 28, 1991
PATENTS

### "A Nicotine Lollipop To Help Smokers Quit"

**Edmund L. Andrews**

" For smokers who find that chewing nicotine-laced gum is not enough to kick their habits, a husband and wife have patented Nic-on-a-stick, ( *Nic Stics*)* a lollipop that they say can better mimic the oral gratification of a long stick of tobacco.

'There's a kind of oral fixation or compulsive kind of behavior that smokers all have in common–the need to put something in and our of their mouths and to repeat this in a very ritualistic way,' said Gloria Mascarelli, a former smoker who patented the lollipop with her husband Robert. The couple, antique dealers who live in Holbrook, L.I. said they came up with the idea after Mr.

Mascarelli suffered a heart attack and could not overcome his addition to cigarettes.

The lollipops, which have not yet been produced,
would feature a nicotine treatment that would be sub-
merged beneath fruit or other flavorings.

Mr. and Mrs. Mascarelli obtained patent 5,048,
544."**

*(Italic correction for inaccurate name quoted in the
paper)

**Reprint permission granted by the New York Times

It is certainly clear to me now that the Lord has
definite plans for my life. I'm sure that the columnist,
Mr. Andrews, is unaware that he is part of the miracle
that God is performing for me. I'm awed by all the
attention God is offering. There are times I feel afraid of
the responsibility. I become tempted to tell God to forget
the whole thing. That's not really true God, I was only
kidding! Seriously, Lord, I know you want me to spread
the word, but I am such an inadequate speaker. You are
making it easy by telling me to hand over the writing of
a book based on these notes to Gloria.

This evening Gloria said that she thinks I'm having a
nervous breakdown. She says that I walk around feeling
that I'm invulnerable. It's not that way at all. I just know
that Jesus is watching over me. That's why, when I had
my heart attack, one that was supposedly massive and
debilitating, I just knew instinctively that the doctors
were wrong.

I confess that tonight I feel a little angry with the
Holy Spirit. Why has He asked me to keep my faith a
secret from Gloria? Why have I been instructed to conceal my journal until a deal with Nic Stics is confirmed?
I don't know how much longer I can keep all this a secret
since Gloria is beginning to think that I'm losing my

mind. Then again, if I just came out and told her all the miracles that God is doing for us, and how I converse with the Holy Spirit, she would probably think I was losing my mind anyway.

Here's a thought that makes me happy. The Holy Spirit has never told me to stop smoking. Another happy thought, Regina is back home and doing well. She surprised me by being at Raymond's house when we were invited over for coffee. She revoked her promise to her doctor about going to a halfway house because she says she needs to be with her family. She flew home while we were at the show. Regina has been invited to stay at Raymond's indefinitely. She doesn't want to do the shows with us and she's worried about causing me stress. It's so like her to be more concerned about me (or anyone else for that matter) when I know how she struggles with her own serious problems every day. Raymond feels confident that his prayers for her will have better results than all the therapy she has had.

Regina insists that she is an atheist. She doesn't believe that God would have given her such a terrible life if He was really there. I'm praying that Raymond will lead her to the Lord, so that Jesus will become her therapist.

Before I close my journal, I have another thought about Gloria's impression that I'm having a nervous breakdown. In a way she is right. I am being broken down by the love and power of the Holy Spirit. He has changed me from a confirmed skeptic to a believer. If I act as if I haven't a care in the world, it's only because I feel His inner comfort. I'm just trying to do what He wants me to do: to keep the journal, obey His laws, and honor Him. I'm not crazy enough to think that He would let me fly if I jumped off a building. I firmly believe in His law of gravity.

## Gloria's comments

*When we found out that Regina had persuaded her uncle to let her stay at his home instead of following her doctor's instruction to go to the halfway house, I had immediate misgivings. I had the opportunity to witness her ups and downs firsthand while Bob was in the hospital. I did not think that her medication was effective.*

*Raymond and Carol had agreed to take her into their home without knowing the seriousness of her condition. I knew there would be problems. Raymond had three of his four children at home, and I feared that Regina's behavior would have a bad effect on them. Yet, Ray felt that God had given him a personal ministry with Regina. I did not presume to tell him otherwise, although the Lord was personally warning me of a potential disaster. Regina did not look the least bit composed and appeared to be slightly disoriented. She had gained an enormous amount of weight in the four months she was away. I knew it was just a matter of time before her bulimic disorder surfaced.*

*I was the only one who appeared be worried. I was tired of trying to explain things to Bob, so I just shut up and hoped that I was wrong. Honestly, I was happy that she was with Ray and Carol and not with us. I was much too concerned with my own problems, particularly with trying to keep Bob's environment free from stress.*

*Bob's son Patrick did spend the summer with us and*

came to the shows to help. He would get bored and disappear for hours. Bob returned to the hotel room one day and found him with a girl. "We were just talking, Dad," he said. At the next show, Bob found him in a remote spot of the lobby with another girl. At age fifteen he was very sexually precocious. I did not like the idea that Bob was getting disturbed by his behavior.

I was very upset with the baby-sitting chores that Bob's former wife had relegated to us. She had refused to take Regina home with her, thinking that her refusal would encourage Regina to stay in the hospital where she was protected from future suicide attempts. Ann's motives were worthy but Regina refused to remain hospitalized and the responsibility for her care fell on us. Although Regina was living with Ray, Bob still felt responsible for her. Now Patrick's care had also become our obligation. My heart just was not in the right place to accept these parental roles joyfully.

Bob was involved with his business, his children and Nic Stics. I told him that I strongly objected to Patrick spending the summer. We had a roaring argument. He told me to shut up, mind my own business and stay out of it. While we were arguing, I'd forgotten all my worries about his recovery. The doctors told me that he needed a peaceful life. Instead, I was causing him even more stress than his children. I felt guilty and angry at the same time.

"Let him do what he wants; stop caring so much. He's selfish; he doesn't love you or even care about the way you feel," Satan whispered softly in my mind.

"I love you and will take care of you, be caring and obedient to your husband. He needs his children and *they need him," said the Lord.*

*"I wish I could just run away from all this turmoil," I thought to myself in my conscious mind.*

*Three wills were competing for my allegiance: the Lord's, Satan's and my own. Life was becoming more and more chaotic.*

*There was another less personal problem I was facing as well. I was still working towards meeting the deadline on our book about Oriental antiques, and I had neither the time or the inclination to continue writing. It is a testament of praise to the Holy Sprit that I cannot remember the details that actually produced and completed the writing of the manuscript. It was if it somehow completed itself on its own. I was just physically there to translate the completed work onto paper.*

*After Bob's heart attack, I do remember asking for and enlisting the aid of antique dealer friends to write about the specialized areas of the book that would have taken me endless hours of research. Some of them disappointed me by not fulfilling their promises or letting me know too late for me to replace them. Others sent in articles that needed extensive revisions. But most sent me copy-ready material that I transferred into the manuscript in the appropriate places. Without their help in our time of distress, the book would never have been finished. Still, I can't remember editing and collating all the material. I am convinced that God propelled me through the mental and physical strain of getting the final copy done.*

*When I received the first copy off the press, and leafed through the many pages of text and pictures, I spontaneously burst into tears. The finished book was like a miracle. It had an existence of its own to which I felt unrelated. The Lord had truly carried me through a time that I could not have managed on my own.*

# Chapter 10

## His Will–Our Way

Bob's journal continued
September 30, 1991,

Earlier tonight, I called Ray to see how Regina was doing and found out that she was in a deep depression, hearing voices and refusing to take her medication. He had been coaxing and pleading for three or four hours, but she adamantly refused. I went over at nine p.m. and she was still refusing to take her pills.

Earlier that evening while Ray and Carol were out, she had cut her wrists badly, and my niece Lisa had helped her to stop the profuse bleeding. Lisa, who was then a candy striper at a local hospital, was planning to become a nurse. She wasn't normally upset at the sight of blood, but she was shaken and repulsed by Regina's wrist slashing. She had found it difficult to stop the bleeding and was frightened by the experience. There were puddles of blood over a wide area of the kitchen floor. She had just succeeded in cleaning up the mess when her parents returned to the house. Ray and Carol were astonished at the amount of bloody towels that were in the washroom. They were proud of Lisa, but sorry that she was left alone to deal with the emergency. Regina apparently needed constant supervision.

At about eleven p.m. Ray and I told Regina that she would have to sleep in the den where we would take turns watching her. I took first watch. I sat with her, witnessing all her pain, listening to her respond to the "voices" that were telling her not to take her medicines. I began to pray silently to Jesus, pleading that He do something to help. "Please, Jesus," I prayed, "please help her to take her medication. You told me a long time ago that she would be fine. Can You please help her now, Lord?" No more than fifteen minutes later, she turned to me and said, "Dad, you stop smoking for a month and I'll take my medicine."

I smiled at her and said, "You know a month is impossible for me, but I'll stop right now and won't smoke all day tomorrow." She replied, "Okay, it's a deal. Then she went to her pocket book, got her pills, and took them immediately. I was grateful and relieved, but at the same time I was asking God why He makes human beings suffer.

Tonight, as I record yesterday's events, I think I've had a revelation. I know that a loving God does not want us to suffer. But, suffer we must because we live in an evil world. The Lord did not plan to place misfortune in man's path, but He did endow man with a free will as his birthright. The right to make choices is as much a part of our inheritance as our corporal bodies. Satan offered the opportunity to sin through his temptation of Adam and Eve in the garden of Eden. They used their free will and chose to disobey God's commandment by eating the forbidden fruit. If the Lord had interfered with their choices, He would be taking back the freedom that He gave us. God did not want human beings to be robots. Therefore, as human beings in the imperfect world we have created, we are subject to the consequences of our disobedience, facing sin and suffering daily.

Though man paved the way to suffering through his own choices, we still blame God for our condition. People lament over poverty, war and inequality. More personally, individuals are struck by the seemingly unfair death of children, the ravages of diseases such as cancer and aids, the martyred deaths of bomb victims and the like. "Why does this happen?", we ask. "Why did You allow this disaster to happen to me or to someone I love? How can I survive the anguish that I feel?"

Adam and Eve as God's free will prototypes allowed tragedy to enter the world via their disobedience. We cannot turn the clock back and undo what they started. Evil and suffering now exist not by God's will, but by the sinful choice of man. But God is merciful and offers us a way out of our misery.

It is our choice to ask God for help or to ignore Him. He is the only One who can elevate our minds above suffering in our amoral impure state. He is the Giver of the "peace which surpasses all comprehension." (Philippians 4:7) That's why the Holy Spirit is called the great Comforter. We can't avoid suffering, but we can cope with it a lot better with God's help. He can give us the faith to hope for a better life with Him when we leave this life, as we all must do eventually.

Death to this life is inevitable, but the promise of a better life in eternity is an open door that God invites us to enter. Once again man is given the opportunity of exercising his free will. We can enter through the door to God's kingdom by choosing to surrender our sin and suffering to Jesus who has already paid the price for our sin by His sacrifice, or we can hold on to our self-righteous notions of self sufficiency and ignore God completely. The price we pay for ignoring God is total separation from His comfort and presence both in this world and beyond. It's a mystery why anyone would not choose Him.

I can't believe I'm saying all this, since I have been guilty of ignoring God for all these years. I was so caught up in myself and in my own ability to handle my life that I left no opportunity to even consider that I needed Him. It must be human nature to just forget about God when everything in our lives is going well. Even now, when I am having a fantastic day, I don't think of Him at all. I don't call out for His help when everything is going well or when I am happy about the events in my life.

Although I was grateful that God had answered my prayer for Regina to take her medication in just fifteen minutes yesterday, I've completely forgotten to thank Him until this very minute when I remembered that I had prayed for His assistance. With all that has happened in the past year or so, I almost passed up recognizing one of God's miracles. It's amazing how easy it is to forget the reality of God's willingness to help us when we pray to Him.

October 2, 1991

I'm very anxious to place our invention with a company who will manufacture it and give us some royalty income. I'm praying to God to speed things up. Patience! I still haven't learned the lesson God has been trying to teach me. I can't believe I'm so stubborn. I have been getting angry and short tempered with Gloria over stupid issues these last few days. I'll have to keep asking for help with this. I thought I was doing better but I'm not.

Here's another thought that reveals some of my confusion. When we were at a show last week, I developed a condition that is commonly called "water on the elbow." I asked a doctor friend what to do about it. He said I would have to have it drained because it wouldn't disappear on its own. I'm asking God to take care of it instead. I know that the condition is not serious, and it can wait. I don't know if God wants me to go to the doctor or if He will cure it for me. With the heart attack, it was hospital loud and clear, but fluid on the elbow? I really don't know. Anyway, I've had enough of doctors and needles. God has been so good to me, I'll just wait and see what He says. Of course Gloria keeps urging me to follow my friend's advise. But then, she doesn't know I'm praying.

October 9, 1991

Sunday night we went to Atlantic City for a little fun and relaxation. While we were driving there, Gloria asked me what I wanted to do with the royalty money we would get from the invention. I said I wanted to be a movie producer. She said she would like to see the money spent on a television show devoted to the miracles that God performs in the everyday lives of people and that we should use the money to spread the love of God. I told her that I wanted to produce more Arnold Swartzenegger movies.

Little did she know that God had given her the same thought that he had given me. From her expression, I gathered that she didn't find my facetious remark funny. If she had looked closely, she would have seen the tears in my eyes, as I thanked Him for her words. Even though Gloria had no knowledge of my plans, God was directing her thoughts to coincide with mine. He was continuing to unite us in a plan to glorify Him together by giving us the same goal. I am deeply touched by the personal attention of the Holy Spirit. I've found that the more I talk to Jesus, the more He reveals Himself to me. So far everything I've asked for has been given. There really hasn't been one prayer that has gone unanswered.

I'm still waiting for the water in my elbow to disappear, but, I state again, He has answered every single need, big or small. I trust Him. I now have a tooth that needs root canal. How much can I ask for? I think He knows how to keep me in line so that I have to keep coming to Him for help.

We are about to offer the Nic Stic patent to several companies. I would like to ask God to get us a contract by December of this year. But, I am still worried that I won't be ready to be a spokesman for Him by then. Instead, I will pray that He teaches me according to His plan. I will try not to worry about things and just leave myself open to follow His instructions.

God has been prompting me to make sure this section of my journal is included in our book. He told me once again, I must not give this journal to Gloria until the licensing contract on Nic Stics is sealed. I don't know why this is so, but, He is in charge. He is leading me, and I will follow. What better way to receive orders than to receive them from God!

I still don't know why He chose me. Yet, it must be true that anyone who asks for faith and believes is capable of receiving an answer to his prayers. What a fantastic God!

October 19, 1991

We just finished doing a local antique show. I didn't pray for any amount. I just left it up to the Lord to decide. We ended up with just a few dollars in profit. I'd asked Him a long time ago just to provide enough for us to get through until our patent started to produce income. So far so good.

I still haven't been able to stop smoking, and I've asked God to help me quit as soon as a contract is signed. The water on my elbow is almost completely gone. I did go to the dentist to have the root canal taken care of. That's one for God, one for the doctor; but who's counting?

Regina is doing very well. That's one less worry that

I have. I am still upset that I can't share everything that is happening with Gloria. I wish I could tell her now, but God said I should take her away for awhile after the contract is signed and let her read the journal at that time. It will be her job to interpret all of this and write a book about prayer.

Still, even with all the evidence, I occasionally feel a small tingle of disbelief. Can this be happening to me? Is it real; is it really God or my imagination? He knows this feeling I have, and He keeps reassuring me. It's just that on some occasions, some evil spirit interjects some doubts that are geared towards taking me away from Him. Right now I feel that I am ninety-seven percent true to my faith in the Almighty. Yet, that little three percent keeps cropping up when things go wrong. As soon as I start talking to Him, the doubts disappear. I wonder if it's possible to be one hundred percent faithful all the time. How do I discard the remainder of my skepticism?

## Gloria's Comments

*At some point between this and Bob's next journal entry, Regina went back to the hospital. Ray and Carol had done their best to help her but her symptoms of hallucinations, voices and self mutilation intensified during her stay at their house.*

*One day, Ray interrupted her as she was cutting her arms with a razor blade. He attempted to grab the blade away from her while she was sitting on her bed, and they ended up in a wrestling match. Regina refused to relinquish the tool that she thought would release her from the voices that were plaguing her. Ray backed away and begged her to return the razor blade. When she wouldn't respond, he offered his own arms and requested that she cut him instead. She continued to slash at her arms. He was not getting through to her. The inner voices that possessed her were the only sounds she heard. Ray grabbed her wrist trying to stop her. She pushed him away with such force that he landed on the bedroom floor. She bolted from the bed and out the front door into the street, razor blade in hand.*

*When he caught up.with her, he finally succeeded in wresting the blade from her hand. Holding on to Ray, she returned to the house sobbing and in distress. Bob's brother was beside himself with anxiety and fear for her safety. Despite all his efforts and prayers, Regina's condition had not improved.*

*Later that day, after consulting with Carol, Ray decided that he could no longer be responsible for Regina's care. Regina's illness had totally dominated the life of his family. His older daughter had been away at college during Regina's stay, but his other three children were upset with the turmoil that Regina created in their environment. Her personal habits, mood swings and need for self-punishment negated their willingness to cooperate with their father's efforts.*

*At first, they were happy to have their cousin with them, united in their efforts to turn her into a happy child. By now, they were tired of having her around and jealous of the attention she was getting. Regina would have to leave. They were all of one mind on the matter. Ray was filled with anxiety, thinking Bob would blame him for his failure. He felt he was letting Bob down.*

*We returned home one day after the incident with the*

*razor blade. Ray immediately called us over for a family conference to tell us what had happened and the subsequent decisions that he and his family had made. He had already told Regina that her behavior indicated that she needed rehospitalization. When we got to Ray's house, Regina was included in our discussion. She had already accepted the decision that Ray suggested.*

*Bob brought up the possibility of her coming to live at our house again. Regina did not think it was a good idea. She was worried about the tension he would feel over her illness. She obviously loved her father very much to sacrifice being with him and to accept a hospital admission instead. I believe that she was relieved to go back to the safety of a hospital. When she lived with a family, the pressure of trying to act normal must have been difficult for her. Recently, she had been trying to hide her bulimia from the us. She would sneak into the bathroom after her meals to throw up. She explained that it had started voluntarily as an effort to lose weight but had become reflexive after a day or two. It had presently become uncontrollable.*

*Regina did, however, have extended periods of time when she felt acceptable to herself and others, usually during the first weeks of a home visit. One of her doctors had described this to us as the "honeymoon effect." During those times she loved to laugh, sing and giggle as much as any other teenager. She was entertaining, charming and had all the qualities anyone would love in a child. It would have been impossible for a stranger to suspect that she had a serious mental illness. Usually, within several weeks of her arrival, she would start to withdraw socially and to spend more time alone in her* room, trying to hide symptoms of her distress that were becoming obvious. At the time of the razor blade incident, she had been staying with Ray's family for forty days and could no longer hide her symptoms from anyone.

She was denied readmission to the Louisiana hospital because she had refused to accept halfway house recommendations. We found a local state hospital that would accept her on her testimony that she felt suicidal. It was not our first choice of hospitals, but it was close and we all could visit her frequently. We hoped that she would be ready to accept a halfway house admission when she left the facility.

# Chapter 11

## One Step Forward, Two Steps Back

Bob's journal continued
June 16,1992

I have not written in this journal for eight months. In January of 1992, I asked God to heal Regina in exchange for the anticipated success of Nic Stics that I'd been promised. At that point I had already been told by several knowledgeable people that the potential sales of such a product would produce multiple millions of dollars of income and at least several million dollars for the patent holder. Even knowing this, I nevertheless asked the Lord to lift Regina's burden rather than grant me success. It was the only sacrifice I had to offer. The invention was the Lord's idea, after all.

Since then we have had no word on Nic Stics, but Regina does seem to be doing better. She stayed with us for five weeks at Christmas time after her release from a local hospital, and I really felt good about having her home in spite of all the concerns we had about watching her behavior. When her symptoms began to surface again, she launched a diligent telephone search, and managed to find another Louisiana hospital that would accept her as a patient. For some unknown personal reason Regina is attracted to living near New Orleans and would not listen to any others suggestions for hospital placement.

It is becoming obvious that Regina can only cope with life outside a hospital for a short time. Yet, I still have hopes, considering the deal I made with God.

It's ironic that I just remembered back to a time before I allowed the adoption to take place. I was accused by my children's stepfather of having offered to give them up for a fee of $10,000.00 each. This juicy tidbit of information was repeated to the court and to my children in an attempt to discredit me once again. The fact that the story was untrue didn't occur to my children or the courts, because I was already branded as an unfit father. Here I am now, in truth, willing to give up all that I feel God has promised to me in exchange for Regina's health. The funny part is that I can't tell anyone about it, not yet anyway.

I had major heart surgery when we were down in Florida in February. It seems that my thallium stress tests had been lost. Six weeks later, in the middle of our show schedule, my doctor who had finally received the results, called our answering machine and left an urgent message. He told me to get to the hospital immediately. Sure enough my angioplasties had failed.

The doctors at Broward General Hospital, who had planned a leisurely Saturday, were forced to come in and perform an emergency triple by-pass. I was told that I never would have made it home without suffering another heart attack. The cold weather would have triggered it.

I went into the hospital, and Gloria decided to do our next show alone because I would be pretty much out of it for a few days. She says she came to the hospital each day after the show, but I really can't remember a thing. Miraculously, they released me only six days after the surgery. I didn't think too much about the whole procedure. It was over so quickly. It wasn't that much of a big deal, I thought. I figured that God would take care of it and He did.

I asked God to find me a new profession. Dealing in antiques is a very unstable and I really felt ready to look for something else. I no longer felt that Nic Stics had a chance after I relinquished it to God in exchange for Regina's healing. Gloria and I proceeded to get involved with two multi-level marketing programs, one following the other. Although we were successful at first, sales began slowing down . We have devoted a lot of physical and emotional energy to getting the business launched, but I'm starting to doubt that they were worth the effort.

I've stopped asking for a specific amount of income at antique shows, and our finances are wrecked. We haven't had a good show in a long time. The problem is that I haven't been staying in touch with God everyday. I guess that is why His fellowship is so important.

We are so far behind financially, I don't know when we will catch up. This time I am asking God for an

$8,000.00 show which seems to be impossible, even with
God taking over, because the economy is so bad. I'm also
again asking God to help us with Nic Stics. Remember-
ing my pact, I am not asking for much now. I'm not one
bit sorry that I made a deal with Him about trading large
sums of money in exchange for Regina's health.

Although I was supposed to stop smoking, I guess I
just don't want to stop. I asked God's help to keep my
habit down to a few cigarettes a day. I'm not sure I asked
sincerely because I'm not doing a really good job. I wish
I didn't enjoy smoking so much. I'm really a smoking
addict, and I know any addiction is a sin.

## Gloria's Comments

*When Bob was hospitalized for his heart surgery we
both felt relief mixed in with the nervous anticipation of
the operation. Living with angioplasties that could possibly close again was not an ideal situation for someone
who was a smoker. Nicotine actually constricts the arteries,
and Bob was still smoking his two to three packs a day.
We both knew that the possibility of another attack was
likely. Just prior to his surgery, the cardiologist made
Bob promise he would give up smoking or he said he
would not proceed with the operation. The promise that
Bob gave was never kept. He managed to rationalize it
away by saying he was under medication when he made
the vow and, therefore, could not be held accountable.*

*Bob stayed in intensive care the night before his
operation. I was told I could call at any time to check on
his status. I could not sleep well alone in our motel
room, so I called the hospital at two a.m. to see how he*

*was doing. I was put in touch with his personal nurse whose conversation with me went something like this:*

*"Oh, Mrs. Mascarelli, I am so glad that you called. I don't know what to do with your husband. He just won't listen to anything I say. I went into his room just a few minutes ago and he was hiding in the bathroom smoking a cigarette with his IV cart and oxygen tank just outside the door. He could have caused an explosion. Please talk to him. If he doesn't behave we won't be able to keep him here. I just don't know what to do. He is such a bad boy."*

*That is exactly what he was. I scolded him accordingly when the nurse put him on the phone. Bob reacted as I had anticipated he would, by laughing and making light of the situation. I knew he would be having surgery shortly, so I did not fully express my negativity about his behavior. I just made sure that I disposed of the cigarettes he had hidden in his clothing before he came back from the operating room the next day. He was so heavily sedated for the next five days that he had no smoking concerns whatsoever. I was sure that a week away from his habit would remove his urge. I was positive that he would recognize the seriousness of the triple by-pass surgery he had just undergone. Surely he would want to avoid any additional blockage he might suffer in the future. He would not want to undergo that operation again.*

*On the morning that he was released from the hospital, Bob said that he wanted to go to a restaurant for breakfast. I thought he should be getting into bed, but he insisted. Thankfully, he did not bring up the issue of smoking at the table. He did however, proceed to order*

127

*a breakfast consisting of bacon, two fried eggs, buttered toast and coffee. Everything he was about to eat had been vetoed by the nutritionist just one day before his release. I was so disgusted by his careless rebellion against medical advise that I got up, walked out of the restaurant and waited for him in our car. Bob had a great breakfast, and I was left hungry and resentful. He was furious with me when he came out.*

*Bob was happy to be angry with me for walking out of the restaurant. He needed someone to be angry with. He was mad about being vulnerable to a sickness that was threatening to take away his pleasures. It was easier to be mad at me and to avoid holding himself accountable for his behavior which he always managed to rationalize away. Bob was, in fact, a master of rationalization. He found excuses for continuing with his unhealthy diet and returning to smoking. Each time I raised the issue of health it would lead to another argument. I quickly learned to stop making an effort to change his lifestyle. I resolutely joined Bob in his attempt to ignore health concerns, and that kept our household free of obvious tension.*

Bob's journal continued
July 3, 1992

Today I thought I heard the Lord affirm that multi-level marketing is the right choice for us. But since I'm not talking to Him as much as I used to, I'm not sure if this was my idea or His. Maybe I'm being influenced by the fact that Gloria learned that the top executives in one of the companies are born again Christians.

Regina is still in the hospital in New Orleans.

Things are not going well at the antique shows, and my last prayer of making $8,000.00 was not answered. We just barely covered our expenses, but we are still surviving. Nic stics seems pretty much dead. We have received lots of rejection letters on our first mailings and have sent out another bunch of letters to other companies. Regina's progress, however, is coming along slowly, but coming along.

July 14, 1992

Things are getting worse. Our last show was a bomb. We are now in the hole to the tune of $9,000.00. If this keeps up we may have to sell the house.

We got a call from an investor a few weeks ago but I don't think it will come to anything. After all, I did make a deal with God; Regina's health for Nic Stics. Nevertheless, I still pray for something from the patent that will enable us to fulfill some of our plans, especially the book and television show.

Boy, when things get bad, we sure remember to pray! It's hard for me to stay on a "high" with God without any fellowship. I can't share anything about my faith with Gloria yet. I even forget to say good morning to Jesus and that is really sad.

I'm losing my battle with smoking. I'm praying to God to take the urge away. I'm sure He's working on it, but I'm too dumb to help. Despite all the faith I have, I still have to honestly want Him to help me. I just have to want Him to help me with everything, and maybe that's a hard thing for me to do. I think I can do it by myself, but it's just impossible. I need Jesus to do it because I'm weak and if He doesn't, I will never be able to quit. I have tried. I need to have more faith and trust him to do it for me. Right now, I'm ready to go upstairs to get my cigarettes. It's incredible how stupid I can be. When the time comes, I just know I won't even want to look at another cigarette.

July 20, 1992

Gloria and I went to a Sequela (reunion) of people who have been on Tres Dias weekends. I met a nice couple there who told me they had given up their jobs to do missionary work, and God had taken care of everything for them. This is another reminder to me to have patience and let God take care of things. I've just got to have faith.

It's amazing. Gloria just told me that she would give up Nic Stics and the potential millions it could bring if only Regina would get better. She was thinking the same thought that I had prayed to God months ago. I know now that we will probably never get our invention off the ground, unless, of course, God decides to give us a little bonus. It, like everything else, depends on Him. The most important issue is that Regina must be healed.

August 10, 1992,

In desperation over our finances, I went out on a job interview but I was told I was too old for that kind of a start-up position. Fortunately, the Lord provided us with a decent income for the last two shows. I don't know why I lose faith so easily. I should realize by now that God will take care of all our needs.

I know I told God that I would give up Nic Stics to have Regina better, and amazingly Gloria had the same thought. Yet, I did change my mind, not about Regina's health, but about a little bonus that God might give us to enable me to go ahead with my plans to work for Him. I will have to keep trying to push Nic Stics in hope of getting this extra income. I hope God knows that I haven't gone back on my deal. Not at all.

I've just started to read the Bible again. The Book of Samuel had some impact on me. If the Lord tells you to do something, even if it is a small task and it is not what you would have chosen, it is best to follow His word and show Him obedience through faith.

God has been telling me not to re-read the past two years of my journal entries until the time comes to write the book about my prayers. I don't know if a lot of what I am writing is repetitious. He also told me to start the writing in Jerusalem rather than Las Vegas which was my choice for a vacation. Las Vegas would have had the advantage of giving me some enjoyable distraction while Gloria was in our hotel room spending hours trying to decipher these writings.

I don't feel too guilty about playing in the casinos, since I only play poker with other players. I don't throw my money away at roulette or craps, where the casino is the only one that benefits in the long run. I like a safe game like poker where I am matching my wits against other players. It's a game of strategy where the risk taking is minimal in a low stakes game. Also, the casino only benefits from taking a small percentage of the pot.

So, if I do lose some money, it goes to another player and not the casino. Many times I win a little. I don't really feel like a gambler. I don't risk money that's needed to pay bills. But, rather than this diversion, my orders are to go to Israel. I can understand that God prefers His holy city to Las Vegas. Ha, Ha! (I have just recognized that the words I wrote represent my attempt to justify gambling to God. I doubt that He would have the same viewpoint that I just expressed about my poker playing.) If we'd only get some kind of extra income from the patent we could get everything moving. How else will I ever get the money for the trip to Israel?

Jesus, I need patience, better understanding of others, and most of all, restraint of anger against my wife Gloria who is probably many times better qualified to work for God than I am.

November 8, 1992

Things are just not going right. I haven't been hearing from the Lord. I've kind of lost touch. I've asked Jesus to answer my prayers and everything is at a standstill. We just finished a show in New Orleans. We'd signed up for it because we would be able to see Regina at the hospital while we were there. We had wishful hopes that she was ready to come home with us, so we had her temporarily released in our care. We already had a halfway house lined up to receive her when we returned to New York. She stayed at her Uncle Richie's house until our show was over. When we went to pick her up for the trip home, she was in such bad shape we had to put her back in the hospital again. Nothing is happening with Nic Stics. The show was a financial disaster!

While we were taking the long ride home, I kept praying for Jesus to give me some reassurance and trying to focus on "hearing" His direction for my life. It occurred to me that there was no reason for Jesus to answer my prayers because I haven't been doing what He asked of me. My patience is lousy, and I'm still smoking, among other things.

I was more than willing to give up my invention's potential for millions of dollars in return for Regina's healing, yet, she is worse. I asked for a small amount of income that would give me the economic freedom to devote time to start writing this book. What happened? Everything is wrong. Where is my message? How about a prophesy or something, Lord?

Later, when we were driving on the New Jersey Turnpike, I decided to turn the radio to a religious channel that I listen to when passing through that area. Sometimes, God presents an answer to something that is bothering me through listening to a radio ministry. It's easy to manipulate Gloria to ask me to turn to religious programming. She always ends up believing that it is her idea.

When I tuned in 570 on my car radio, there was a religious program, but its subject was nutrition. This isn't an area that interests me and besides, it didn't seem to apply to the questions that I had just proposed to the Lord. I was just about to change the stations when just ahead, I saw a tower, with the letters WMCA 570 at the top. At that moment I heard Jesus say, "Listen. Do not change stations."

Within the next fifteen minutes there was a program change. At five-forty p.m. on station 570 there was a program titled "Confidence in Prayer."

The minister's message said have faith, ask for realistic goals, believe God will answer, and ask him for proof if you wish. Believing that Jesus had given me the direction to take, I then prayed for the following, asking for specific goals in my prayer: Regina was to be better in the next six to twelve months; Nic Stics was to be sold in the next two months, providing a small income that would enable the book to be written; Regina, Valerie, Cheryl and Cindy would have a singing group (no time limit); we would start a television show devoted to answers to prayer (no time limit).

I have no doubt that hearing this radio program was not a coincidence, even though the odds are probably the same as me drawing to an inside royal flush in poker. God doesn't play the odds. He performs miracles. So, why am I not getting excited because God spoke to me again? What stops me from showing my strong emotions when I am touched by God? Am I starting to take Him for granted?

I believe this will probably be the last entry in this book if Jesus doesn't bring about the Nic Stics income so that it can be written. Right now I feel that everything will be accomplished as He promised. Why can't I feel this way all the time? Of course, no matter what happens, I'll write again to note that Regina is well and on her way to full recovery.

Thank you Jesus, that this book is supposed to be written or started in Jerusalem. Amen!

**(Gloria's note:** *Bob signed his name under the word Amen.)*

November 11, 1992

I received four calls on possible appointments for Nic Stics today. Regina called to say that she is going into a new program. She sounded terrific and even said that she is looking forward to going into a halfway house after she completes it. She sounds enthusiastic.

November 14, 1992

Regina called today to say she's started in her new program. I asked her if she was finally going to get to work on getting well, and she answered that she was working on it. I asked her about hearing voices and she replied that she hadn't heard them lately. I wanted to know if she had gotten rid of her "ghost" friend Fred, and she answered that he wouldn't leave until she got better. She said that she still needed him now. I pressed her by asking when she thought she'd be able to leave Fred. She replied that it would be within six months to a year, possibly sooner. It was the first time that Regina gave me an answer about getting well.

Gloria was sitting next to me while I was having this conversation. I wanted to turn to her and share my enthusiasm about how quickly God was answering my prayers, but I can't tell her anything yet, even though I feel like I'm going to explode.

I have no idea why I signed my name to my last entry. I guess it's because I thought that I was finished with my writing, but by giving me hope with Nic Stics and Regina's progress, He has given me reasons to go on.

Gloria had picked Israel as a vacation site if we got money from Nic Stics and then changed her mind, anticipating we would be going in the rainy season (December through February). Well, she changed her mind back again after watching a program about Israel, so I'm interpreting this as an optimistic sign that we will be going there as part of God's plan.

I've been telling her that I have a new project to discuss when we get to Israel, and that she mustn't tell anyone about it until it is accomplished. Imagine having a woman keep a secret like this for a year or so? It will really be a challenge for Jesus to keep her quiet. I can just see her exploding with the news of my secret journal and telling everyone that she is going to write a book about it.

November 18, 1992

Regina is doing very well and is finally ready to accept the plan for her to go on to a halfway house or community living after her hospitalization. Finally, after four years she is ready to take recovery seriously.

Imagine, tomorrow I have an appointment with a representative of a pharmaceutical house about the invention.

November 26, 1992

Regina is doing great! Her Uncle Richie says that this

is the best he has ever seen her. Even Gloria says that there's been a great change. She thought it might have been a result of her conversation with Regina telling her she had the power to correct the path of her life. I wanted to correct Gloria and tell her that she was wrong. Jesus has done it all, because He had made that promise to me.

On the other hand, Nic Stics was not accepted by the drug company. I am making one last prayer for another drug company to come through before the sixty days are up. I figure that I have about a forty percent chance of it going through. Why I have any doubt at all is amazing since this is Jesus' idea. So why does my vision sometimes get so clouded? Do I think that He is going to change the game plan? My prayers were specific and His answer has seemed to be that everything is taking place on schedule.

November 31, 1992

Crash! I just found out that our last hope for the invention seems dead. It looks like our plans to get to Jerusalem and write the book about prayer are finished.

Crash! I just found out that after spending just one week in a community house, Regina has been thrown out and is being put back in the hospital.

Crash! I had to go back into the hole and borrow money to buy merchandise. Our stock was very low and we were living off our inventory without replacing anything.

Crash! I had an argument with Gloria. Last week I was her brilliant husband and today I don't know how to buy the right antiques to make money. I picked the wrong antique co-op to place merchandise in and I never finish what I start, including Nic Stics.

Patrick, who has been living with his mother, quit school yesterday. I think I managed to talk him into going back; my bonus event in a week of disappointments.

What is the expression about the Lord not giving us more than we can bear? Now what? Well, I guess these disappointments are not more than I can bear. I can probably bear some more, but why? Oh well, this was God's idea right from the beginning, so I'm going to let Him handle it all.

Gloria is worried about all the friends to whom I'd promised some of the royalties. She blames me for having stirred up vain hopes. I'm not too upset about that since I know that they are used to my flops and can laugh with me about them with as much good humor as if they'd received a profit. I am disappointed, however, because I wanted to start being a soldier for God, and I wanted to start tomorrow. I guess He figures I'm not ready yet. I know it's not because I'm not worthy, because if I was completely hopeless He would not have started any of this to begin with.

December 9, 1992

This weekend Gloria and I were discussing prophesy, and she brought up religion and the signs that come from God. I then asked her to ask for a sign from God about Regina. She refused. I insisted. It became a little game we were playing. I told her that since she was a believer, and I was a doubting Thomas, she alone had the right to ask Jesus for a sign. She said that it really was possible to get a sign from the Holy Spirit. I said "Fine, check with Him." Anyway, on the way home from our show Sunday night, at three or four o'clock in the morning, a radio program came on discussing the Holy Spirit. I, of course, immediately thought that this was God's way of letting me know that there is still hope for our patent.

I wanted to talk about the topic of signs from the Lord with Gloria because I hoped that she had some insight about the sale of the patent. Would we have it sold in sixty days? Prior to this, we met with a woman who had assured us that she was working on a deal for us and that we would have a closing date on Monday or Tuesday. Well, today is Wednesday and nothing is happening. I still feel doubt although it is probably only registering at the 10% level.

I should be 100% confident. Maybe I'm letting the world around me interfere with my faith. For instance, someone gave me an article this Saturday, which showed that the statistics of any invention making it to the marketplace were .01 of 1%. There are unbelievable odds against me. This fact, added to the failure of receiving a phone call regarding a closing date, has made me cautious.

God has told me not to re-read anything that I have written in the past couple of years, and I am resisting that temptation. The only time I will have a full view of what I've written is after a full contract is signed, and I help Gloria write this book. I wish I could peek back to see if everything I wrote is coming true. I wonder if I keep repeating myself.

Oh boy, this sounds crazy, but Jesus just told me to forget about taking a lap top computer to Israel. I'm just to bring a tape recorder to record all the questions and answers I will share with Gloria about my journal. I did say a prayer that our last show would get us through the holiday season, because it will be our last until 1993. It turned out to be twice as good as last year.

December 20, 1992

We still have no definite word about a closing date. Believing that God will answer a specific prayer at a specific time is tough. I find that I don't have perfect faith. I can understand if God doesn't answer me.

Some people ask God to perform a miracle for them in exchange for promises they make, vowing to give up sins like drinking, lying or cheating in return for God granting whatever they've asked for. If individuals succeed in relinquishing their sins in return for God's favor, they generally end up giving credit to themselves for giving up their bad habits. Their friends and family inevitably compliment them as well. People praise them for their success, crediting them with the will power to overcome their weakness.

In cases like this, God's involvement gets lost. The prayer helps the individual if it is answered and the person may have lived up to his end of the bargain. But, it is the individual who is exalted before his friends and family, not God. Answers to prayer really should result in God's glorification.

God, please answer my prayers, and I promise to glorify You. I will tell people what You have done for me. I will do all things according to Your will. I will help my neighbor as I would have You help me, giving all credit to Your name. I will continually seek to do what glorifies You.

December 27, 1992

Well, we received a business plan and a preliminary licensing agreement. There may just be a chance of this going through after all. We will just have to wait and see. Regina's progress seems to have slipped back somewhat, but God has promised she will be healed. I won't worry about her. She is in His hands and has been for a number of years now.

Our lawyer says that our deal for a licensing agreement only has one chance in a thousand of going through, yet the broker says that we will have a settlement date by the end of January. At least some hope is still alive within the time frame I prayed for.

January 20, 1993

I've had another sign that God is still very much involved with my prayers. Valerie called from Canada and mentioned that she would love to come back to New York to start a singing group with her two step-sisters.

There have been several times the Holy Spirit has filled me with complete peace. When I've been overly anxious about the patent, I've prayed for Him to take away the feelings of tension and anxiety, and He has brought feelings of comfort and optimism to me. I've felt a warmth flow through me that I can only compare to the safety an infant must feel when cuddled in its mother's arms. It's a physical sense of relaxation, a safe comfort that enables worries and fears to disappear in seconds.

In the middle of anger, frustration and worry, it is not easy to immediately turn to God and ask for release. When I'm overwhelmed with worldly emotions, I lose sight of God who is still by my side just waiting for me to turn to Him for help. I'll have to remember to seek Him quickly on days when I feel things are about to go wrong. I must remember to thank Him on days when things are going well. I must always remember to keep Him foremost in my mind!

# Chapter 12

## Dad, I Went to Church Today

**Gloria's comments**
March 1993

*Whenever I thought about Regina, I pictured her as a tortured soul. Regina's depression was clinical. Along with it were the added diagnoses of manic depressive disorder, schizoaffective disorder, personality disorder, bulimia, and more. If a mental disease existed, Regina was diagnosed as having had it at one time or another. Although there were many times we laughed together, both on the phone and during her visits, I knew that her moments of levity were only a temporary brightening in an otherwise continually distressed state of mind. Also, I honestly believed that there were times she actually welcomed the symptoms of her mental illness because she felt that she was not worthy of living a normal life.*

*The source of Regina's unrelenting depression lay in*

her memories. *She could not escape from the flashbacks of abuse caused by a man that she had been told was her "good Daddy"; the man who told her he would kill her family if she ever revealed the truth.*

*Because of the nature of Regina's disorders, no one could substantiate whether some of Regina's memories were, in reality, fact or hallucination. Regina insisted that her adoptive father had repeated raped and brutalized her when she was barely a teenager. She claimed that he had told her that she was stupid and useless except when she used her body to satisfy his sexual desires. Regina said that her feelings of worthlessness led her to promiscuity and drugs. Regardless of whether some or all of these memories were true or not, Regina viewed them as real. She was haunted by them continually, as her voices assailed her, echoing the phrases of her insignificance and unworthiness.*

*I saw Regina's weariness with living and understood it. My heart was distraught at her helplessness despite everyone's efforts to heal her. I hardly knew how to treat her when she was with us. Some of the time I felt I would die for her well-being. At other times I wished she would return to the hospital.*

*As I was driving alone in my car one day in late February, I started to think of how hard life was for Regina and those who loved her. She was still in a New Orleans hospital. Bob, the optimist, kept imagining that she was getting better and talked about taking her home once again.*

*I knew that she was not making any progress. She still cut her wrists superficially as a means of self punishment and she refused to accept advise on another halfway house placement. Regina had been tossed out of the last one because she had been seen drinking by a patient and was sexually involved with another. She knew that kind of behavior would get her thrown out, but she chose to break the rules, perhaps subconsciously thinking that her rebellion would get her back to the hospital where she felt safe.*

*I knew that she required hospitalization, yet Bob wanted her back home again with us. He did not recognize that each time she failed at living in a normal family situation, she ended up feeling even worse about herself. She was living in a downward spiraling whirlpool, stuck in the vortex, and no other human being, no matter how caring, could reach her to pull her out.*

*As I was driving along, thinking about the insurmountable problems surrounding Regina, I realized that everyone in our family, except for Bob, had some negative feelings about this tortured girl. We were overwhelmed by her ongoing self destructive behavior. We feared another suicide attempt. All of us had expressed anxiety at the thought of having her come home again. We were reluctant to deal with the stress of watching her behavior. We hated the residual feelings of both pity and guilt when she would again have to be hospitalized after another crisis.*

*I suddenly got the thought of what a relief it would be if Regina really did succeed in committing suicide. I thought, for a moment, that this would be the perfect solution to everyone's problems. Regina would be freed from her misery. Bob might avoid having another heart attack. I could stop worrying about taking Regina back without hope of her getting better. Her siblings and cousins could stop feeling guilty about avoiding her because of their growing repulsion towards the symptoms of her illness. In my mental state of free associated thinking, I did not immediately recognize how horrible my thoughts really were.*

*As I continued my musings during the drive, I started to think of what life would really be like without Regina. True, the worries about her welfare would all be gone but, how would I honestly feel if I knew that I would be cut off from her permanently in this life?*

*My mind then switched track to positive thoughts. I began thinking about Regina's positive attributes and how they related to me and my family. I thought about her sweetness, how she always cared about my feelings and how happy she was each time she was released to our care from a hospital. I remembered how much she enjoyed the simple things that we took so much for granted, like eating a favorite food that she had no access to, or having a new experience that her hospital confinements kept her from. I thought of her childlike innocence, despite all that had been done to her and all that she had done.*

*I recalled the time I sat at the foot of her bed and we talked. How surprised I was when she started to laugh with pleasure at the simple intimacy we had established by this ordinary act of communication. "This is so great," she said. "You're just sitting here and talking to me. It's so normal. This is so great," she repeated as she bounced on the mattress with enthusiasm. I started to cry as I pursued these thoughts. How I would miss her if she was gone!*

*If Regina succeeded in committing suicide, I certainly*

146

would be free of all the anxiety and feelings of hopelessness, but I would be losing a very special girl whom I now called daughter. As I continued this train of thought, I realized for certain, that I wanted Regina to live. I wanted her to be here with us so that I could continue to love her. The struggle that I had been feeling earlier now vanished. Regina was definitely worth more to me alive with all her problems than any relief I would feel from the burden of caring for her. I wanted her to live, regardless of all the difficulties. I even wanted her to come home again. God let me know that.

As I look back I now realize that God allowed me to have my negative thoughts for a reason. He had allowed me to imagine Regina's death so that I could learn to recognize how important she was to me. He gave me pause to consider the depth of my love for her. I had received a moment of revelation that reassured me that I truly loved Regina to the point of selflessness. If He had not done just that, I would not have had any preparation for what was about to happen. As God often does, He gave me this realization just at the right time.

The day before Regina finally succeeded in her efforts to be free of her pain, she called Bob. It was a Sunday afternoon. I was not around for the call but Bob told me later that Regina had called to say, "Dad, I just want you to know that I went to church today." This was important news! Regina strongly professed that she did not believe in God. "How could He be real and let all those horrible things happen to me?" she had said more than once. "I believe in the Devil," she would say.

But, on this particular Sunday, March 7, 1993, Regina went to church. Something important had led her there, *and she called her father to let him know that she had gone. This phone call was the key to the veiled door of knowledge that would slowly open over the next weeks.It marked the beginning of a sequence of events that would have to be carefully interpreted to reveal the full message of God's plan concerning Regina. Discernment would help to unravel the intent of the signs and wonders God would bring to our lives. Wisdom and knowledge would become our companions. Peace and joy would become our reward.*

Monday, March 8, 1993

*It started out as a lazy ordinary day. Bob and I watched morning TV together, expecting Patrick and his friend to come by for a pizza at dinner time. When I went upstairs to take two 20 mg Lasix pills that were kept in Bob's medicine cabinet, I had no idea that my day would be far from commonplace, and that its events would become etched in unforgettable detail in my mind.*

*My pills were stored in an ordinary brown medicine container smaller than any others in the cabinet. Regina's tranquilizers, identical in size and shape, were stored in a similar bottle and kept (I thought) on a shelf in her room. Her room was generally undisturbed when she was gone. Regina's medication had been apparently misplaced in our medicine chest, because I ended up taking two strong tranquilizers, thinking that I had taken two benign diuretic pills.*

*When I first began to feel woozy, I had no idea it was related to the medication. Bob suggested that I recheck the label on the medicine bottle when I told him how I*

148

*felt. The logo on the pills looked unfamiliar, so I called Raymond at his pharmacy to check out the inscription. Ray told me that I had just taken a double dose of Regina's medication, and that I should expect to be "zonked out" for most of the day. He also assured me that I was in no danger. Feeling apprehensive however, I decided to collapse on the den sofa where Bob could keep an eye on me.*

*As predicted, I was passed out on the sofa until long after Pat arrived and dinner was over. When I did awaken, I was still much too relaxed to function normally. I went to the refrigerator looking for some sugary food for a quick pick-me-up. Pat and his friend were upstairs and Bob was down in his office where he was working on his stamp collection. I heard the phone ring but I ignored it. I was unable to move quickly, and I knew that Bob was at his desk.*

*The next thing I remember was the sound of Bob running up the stairs. I noticed his reddened face. He looked as if he had been laughing uncontrollably. I expected him to tell me something funny. Instead he blurted out the name Regina, and grabbing me in a fierce embrace, he began to sob. As dull as I was feeling, I knew from the moment he said her name, that Regina was gone. "Oh no," I said, without feeling any emotion. "Who called?"*

*Regina's uncle Richie was on the phone, calling from Louisiana. I picked up the extension in the den as Bob headed back downstairs. I thought he would pick up the phone, but he did not. I could hear him crying in his office while I heard some of the details concerning Regina's death. Regina died earlier that afternoon. She*

149

had used an institutional bed sheet thrown over a water pipe in the shower room to hang herself. Hospital regulations required an attendant outside the shower room but no one knew how the bed sheet had gotten there. Regina had been searched before entering. After a one hour attempt to resuscitate her, the ambulance attendants had pronounced her dead. She left no note.

I still did not feel any emotional impact from the news, but I was now alert enough to know what had to be done. I immediately called my daughter Cindy who lived near Regina's mom. Ann was home alone and she would need someone to be with her when she heard the news. Cindy threw down the phone when I told her, and Sonny, my future son-in-law, picked up the conversation. With Cindy crying in the background, I told him to meet us at Ann's house. Then I called my older daughter Cheryl who I left distraught as I hung up the phone to go and tell Patrick the news. I asked Pat's friend to leave because I did not want him to be embarrassed by what I knew would be an emotional scene. When his friend left he said, "I know you have something important to tell me, but I'm not sure I want to hear it."

"It's about Regina," I said.

"She's dead," he replied.

I nodded in response as he asked, "Suicide?"

I nodded again as he lowered his head. I went to sit beside him and held him as he quietly started to cry. He did not respond to my embrace. He was as limp and alone in his grief as Bob was. I took Pat by the hand, and we joined Bob who was sitting in his office with tears streaming down his face. No one spoke for several minutes. I broke the silence by explaining what I had done to notify the family and to get help for his ex-wife. The phone rang, and it was Ann herself, who had just been told by her brother Richie that Regina had died.

Shocked and hysterical, she kept insisting that Regina was okay and that Richie was deliberately lying to her. I had to tell her what had happened again, thereby giving Bob and Patrick who were seated nearby, some of the details of information that I had received from Richie. I informed her that she should expect Cindy and Sonny to arrive at her house shortly, and that I was bringing Patrick home immediately.

I was sympathetic to all the painful emotions of that night, although I was merely an observer and not party to them. I was unable to feel any sensitive emotion due to the residual effects of Regina's tranquilizers, yet my ability to reason remained clear. I instinctively felt that I was elected to take charge of the necessary details that could not be handled by the distressed people around me. I wanted to comfort Bob as much as I could, trying to reach him through the blanket of grief that covered him, but I personally felt little surprise or grief of my own. Later, I would conclude that I did not take Regina's powerful tranquilizers by accident but that God had deliberately assigned to me the role of detached care-taker that night.

On our trip home alone in the car, Bob told me through bouts of crying that he wanted everything in the house that belonged to Regina to be removed immediately, and that he was counting on me to get the job done as soon as we got home. He said he could not bear to see her things around the house. He was shocked, angry and not thinking clearly. I disobeyed his request by just removing obvious things to her room and locking the door. I hid all her photographs along with the little gifts that she had given us.

I spent the rest of that night calling others in the family and trying to soothe Bob who was beyond the reach of my comfort. He has stated since that the pain he felt was physical and so intense that it even surpassed the pain of his heart attack. He said it was a physical anguish that's reserved for a grieving parent, intensified by the shock of sudden death. His expectation had been to nurse her into health with his generous unconditional love. She had attempted suicide so many times before that he had stopped taking it seriously. He was fooled into thinking that her unsuccessful suicide attempts were really only a bid for attention.

My thought that night was that Regina's death would forever ruin Bob's life and that he would never recover from losing her. In truth, had I known Bob was a believer, I would have appealed to his faith in God as a solace for his pain. He has since told me that reaching out to the Lord during those first hours of despair did not even occur to him. His faith in God was eclipsed by his grief. He had forgotten completely that he had a Holy Resource to tap into.

*March 9, 1993*

The day was filled with the decisions and plans that always accompany an unexpected death. Cindy left her apartment to come home and stay with us. We had to handle things between our home and New Orleans where Regina's suicide was being investigated and *funeral decisions were being made. I was certainly feeling personal grief by this time, but I seemed to be the only one keeping everyone else organized, so I ignored my own need for comfort.*

*At dinner time I knew I would have to find some food to serve to Bob and Cindy who were both still teary and consoling one another in the den. As I started to open the refrigerator door, my eyes landed on the one item associated with Regina that I had overlooked the night before.*

*It was a crayon drawing that I had attached to the refrigerator with decorative butterfly magnets. Regina had drawn it at my request when I had asked her to show me a picture of her "hallucination" butterflies. When her medications were not effective she often saw them. They were so real to her that members of the family had seen her trying to catch them to save in a jar. The picture that she'd composed, showed five butterflies of different colors all flying up from the ground towards a sunlit sky.*

*As I suddenly discovered the drawing, my immediate thought was that I had failed in my job of hiding Regina's things from Bob's sight. Immediately after that idea, a completely unbidden thought flashed through my mind. It was a thought that asked a question of this simple drawing and of its artist. "Which little butterfly are you, Regina, ascending so beautifully up to heaven?" I questioned silently. My eyes were drawn to the butterfly on the left which seemed to have been drawn with Regina's blond hair. At that instant the full impact of her death hit me and bent me over in an agony of loud heaving gasps of pain and tears. Bob came running into* the kitchen and held me up as I loudly sobbed out my heartache with all the intensity that he had done the night before.

When I recovered enough to speak, I said the words that would be God's healing balm to my husband, words that would wrest the grief from his being as quickly as it had overcome him. I made a simple statement. It was really designed for Bob, delivered through me and received through the knowledge that Bob and the Holy Spirit shared. The words were, "Well, at least we know now that Regina is finally _healed_."

There was no way for me to know the significance that these words would have to Bob. I was unaware of the bargain that he had made with the Lord. I did not know that he had been praying repeatedly that Regina would be healed and that he had stated his willingness to give up all the benefits that would come from Nic Stics' potential profits in return for the answer to his prayer. I did not know that he prayed at all.

His prayers had used the word "heal" specifically. He wasn't praying for Regina to be "made well," to "recover" or to "feel better." He assumed that her healing would accomplish all of those things. When he heard my words saying that she had been healed, the Holy Spirit informed him immediately that this was the way that God had answered his prayer. He knew all at once, in that moment of revelation, that this was the way God chose to lift Regina from her misery. In a flash Bob saw the torture she suffered in her everyday existence and that God had indeed "healed" her by removing her from her earthly pain.

As I looked at Bob, following my statement, I saw his

*eyes sparkle and the corners of his mouth turn up as he said to me. "You're right. She really has been healed. She's all right now."*

*Although I knew nothing of Bob's journal and his growing personal faith, I intuitively felt that my husband had just received an insight from the Lord. His face revealed the blessing of inner peace that only God could have provided at that terrible time of grief. Without knowing any details, I discerned that the Lord had just taken away Bob's deepest pain and that he was going to be all right.*

Bob's journal continued
March 10, 1993

...and I guess best of all, Regina Theresa Mascarelli is completely healed. She is with God and her torment and trouble here are all over.

She went with Him on March 8th, 1993. I am sad, but only because I thought she would be healed in this world. I don't know why God didn't heal her in this life, but I have enough faith to believe that He will tell me the answer in due time.

Regina was so special. I know that God has wonderful plans for her. She has helped us as best she could while she was here by caring for our welfare and trying to protect us from the hardships of her illness. Now she's gone on to better happy days in heaven.

Through her we learned charity and how to perfectly love imperfect people. We discovered how to rest in God's will and not our own. We were schooled in the exercise of patience and deep empathy. She brought a family back together again by insisting that Valerie contact us. She enlightened her brother Pat to the fact that I had never had the chance to prove my love for them after my divorce, making it possible for him to again relate to me as his father. Through her illness we learned to depend on God more and more as we realized our own inability to help. We learned to be less judgmental. There were circumstances beyond her control that lead Regina to mental illness and sin. We have absorbed Christ's lesson through her trials and learned to pity the sinner rather than be judgmental of people who are unpleasantly different from us.

After all that Regina suffered, she really deserves the best. I am going to miss talking to her every day and listening to her funny jokes, and that is really what is making me sad. She was truly a special child, anointed by God to teach us about love. The Lord, in His own way, has fulfilled His promise and has healed Regina forever. I know I'll still shed some tears for her because of my own selfishness, but so what! I think God will forgive me for that.

March 19, 1998

This has been the most fantastic week. I never would have thought I could get through it. I even told Gloria to get rid of everything Regina owned last Monday night. Tuesday started out to be just as agonizing, but, by that night, I was totally reassured that Regina was well and safe. That first day I was sure that I would not even go to the memorial service, but when the time came I was so filled with comfort that it became a celebration of Regina, rather than a source of more pain.

### Monday March 8th

The strange and wondrous events started with Gloria accidentally taking Regina's medication on the day we got the news. She was so totally relaxed that she was able to handle all the immediate details and arrangements that I was incapable of handling.

### Tuesday

Gloria delivered God's message of Regina's healing. I did not know until later that week that butterflies are a Christian symbol for resurrection. How fitting that they were the focus of Regina's hallucinations and served as a message to me that she was healed at last.

### Wednesday

My daughter Valerie arrived. She left here only two weeks ago after a short visit. My ex-wife's parents also came and stayed here. It was Valerie's first opportunity to see them since she was ten years old. Valerie's Uncle Richie called to say he would be flying in with Regina's ashes the next day.

### Thursday

Valerie and her uncle had a very tender reunion after all those years of separation. Richie arrived with many blessings in tow. He told us of some extraordinary experiences he'd had since Regina died, experiences which he could only interpret as messages from God. The most outstanding story took place the day after Regina's death.

He said that he was feeling miserable, but that the family had to eat, so he had reluctantly gone out to shop for some food. As he walked out of a neighborhood fish store with a package in his arms, a car pulled up in front of him and a very large African-American man came running from it, directly to him. Richie is a big man. He is about 6'1" and has just lost some of the bulk that kept him up at about 250 pounds. Rich said this man was big enough to scare him. He must have been 6'3" and weighed about 260 pounds. The man was heading straight towards him with an intense look that was frightening. Richie's first reaction was to move out of his way but he didn't have time to react before the man grabbed him by the arm, pried open the fingers of his free hand, inserted a piece of paper and said, "These words will be a comfort to you in your grief." The man immediately returned to his car and drove away before Richie even had a chance to react to the situation. The folded piece of paper contained a Bible verse, Proverbs 16:22.

> "Understanding is a wellspring of life unto him that hath it: but the instruction of fools is folly." (Authorized King James Version)

Although I could not personally identify with the message, the remarkable method of its transmission left me feeling the same way that Gloria had in Baltimore the year before, that an angel had been involved.

Richie really was supposed to come the day before, but he'd arrived at the airport too late for his flight. To avoid the road construction that delayed him, his friend drove him on a different route that morning. The new direction led them through a poor section of government housing on the way to the airport. As they passed a building that was being sand blasted to clean up graffiti, Richie looked up to the upper two stories that had not yet been cleaned. In two story high letters, in bold red, was the single word, "Regina."

Richie also brought a poem that was given to him by an attendant at the mental hospital after he had returned there, at Gloria's request, to pick up a jacket that we had given to Regina when she first had "happy feet" and ran away from the hospital.

As a reward for good behavior a group of hospital children had been taken to a local movie theater as a treat. Regina, with the help of two friends, had succeeded in running away, and failing to reach us at home, had called her Uncle Ray to pick her up. I remember how Regina giggled when she told all of us about the title of the movie she had gone to see with the hospital group. It was "The Three Fugitives."

We were so happy to see her away from the hospital that we celebrated by buying her a short black leather jacket that was embellished with tassels and fringes. The jacket accompanied her in and out of institutions from that day forward. She treasured it. Gloria told Richie to do what he wanted with her other clothes, but that we wanted the jacket back.

After he left the hospital building with the jacket, a nurse came running out to give him a copy of the poem that had been written for Regina by one of the other patients. The woman who wrote it was told that Regina was transferred to another hospital, not that Regina had died.

We met this patient, Alaina, when we last had taken Regina home with us. She was a very heavy African-American woman who appeared to have had a limited education. At least that was our impression of her, because she expressed herself to us in the following way:

"Take good care of that child, you hear. She gonna die you don't take good care. I loves that child. I gonna cry if she die. You take good care of that child. I gonna cry if she die."

Alaina was particularly concerned about Regina's recurrent bulimia problem, and wanted to make sure we would not allow Regina out of our sight after she ate, in case she tried to throw up her food.

There is no chance that it was anyone other than Alaina who wrote the poem. She was the only large black lady in the ward who had a cast on her leg when we were there in November. That is how Richie reminded us of the identity of the woman who wrote the poem. What we received by her hand was both touching and elegant. It said:

"FOR REGINA"

"The pain enveloped her like a cloud
And the shedding of tears was not allowed
The scars were a river running deep
The horrible memories hers alone to keep

Running away was all she knew
Letting go she could not do
When the anguish was more than she could bear
She took herself away from here
She touched us all within our hearts
Her purpose in life from the very start
Enabling us to cry the tears
We'd held inside for many years
Trying recovery time and again
*Only God could <u>heal</u> the child within* *
Loving her was easy, that we know
The hardest part is letting go"

* (Italics and underlining mine)

## Gloria's Comments

*Those words seemed to have been expressly written for our family. A Divine Force had to be behind the expression of the very essence of Regina's tragedy. Only a Supreme Intelligence would know how to soothe us with the miracle of those poignant words. From our exposure to Alaina's limited vocabulary, I concluded that what she wrote was a reflection of God's inspired thought.*

*Alaina had not written for our eyes or comfort, but the Lord saw to it that her poem reached us, and that it conveyed a message of His will in Regina's passing. Miraculously Alaina had used the word "heal" in a context that fit in perfectly with what the Lord had revealed to Bob. Her reference to Regina's purpose in life as a mission to touch people's hearts was also part of both Bob's and my own revelations.*

*It is not surprising that two of God's important*

*messages to our family were delivered by black people. African Americans were very special to Regina. The black attendants at the hospitals had often become her friends and she had received genuine loving concern from them as they took care of her. Over the years many attendants and nurses had told us how much they loved her and wished they could take her home to care for her personally.*

*Cindy went home briefly to get a copy of the song she had written for Regina when she had first made contact again with our family four years earlier. Cindy had written and recorded it for Regina as a welcome, but when it was played at the memorial the words seem to be perfectly appropriate as a final goodbye to Regina. God had put another miracle in place for our comfort long before it would become appropriate for a memorial service. The title of the song, written five years earlier, was "You're Home Now."*

*All the occurrences of the week following Regina's death seemed to be planned ahead of time by the Master, designed to give us comfort, lift our spirits, and fill us with amazement at the depth of His love.*

Bob's journal continued

Friday

Our home was really filled with the Holy Spirit. The heightened emotional state of sadness mixed with gratitude for our mutual love and support of one another, really welcomed Him into our home in a powerful way.

We had lots of people sleeping at our house. Many of

us stayed up all night talking, twenty-four hours a day, and all of it was Spirit-filled. Ray's children stopped by several times, filled with grief and guilt, and Gloria has ministered to them with a power that can only be gotten from the Holy Spirit. I just don't know how she managed to keep the house going, put food on the table, get laundry done, and give comfort and love to everyone who was needy. She hadn't complained once, or shown any fatigue at all.

### Saturday

This was supposed to be the day of Regina's memorial but, because of the local "blizzard of 93," it was postponed to Sunday. We all laughed thinking about how Regina would enjoy the fun of the unusual snow storm messing up the plans. We all stayed indoors and spent another day of quality time together.

Valerie and her Uncle Richie stayed up all night. Richie confessed his guilt at failing to recognize her plight when she was victimized by her adoptive father.His last memory of Valerie had been as a ten year old child looking at him (with what he now thought to be pleading eyes) from the top of the staircase when he was refused entry into his sister's home. His reaction to this rejection was to never to try to go back again. Years later he moved to New Orleans and this was the first time he had seen his niece in ten years. He blamed himself for not fighting for visitation with the children.

Valerie, touched by his concern for her, and the tragedy that led to her sister's death, began to talk more freely than she ever had about her own childhood experiences. She revealed facts of her abuse that had been hidden for many years. We all cheered her efforts to deal with her past, with a support that was sustained by the desire to see her conquer the feelings of degradation that had just destroyed Regina.

Sunday

Gloria and I carried Regina's ashes to the funeral home for the memorial service. All the way to the chapel, we kept our hands clasped together atop the box placed between us on the front seat of our car. Gloria arranged a memorial table near the pulpit with several pictures of Regina that we had enlarged for that day. The poem written by Alaina was put on the table next to the ashes. Gloria had written a background story for the minister which read:

> "Regina was to all of us, especially to her mother and father, a very special child. She had a sweetness and innocence at the core of her being that touched the most loving part of all of us as well as other people she met in the course of her many hospitalizations. Although Regina suffered through the terrible ordeals of her mental illness, she tried her best to keep those hurts from the ones she loved.
> When she felt well and able to meet the strains of life, she always managed to gain release from the hospital and come to live with one of us. When she was with us she enjoyed the love and caring of a full family life. When her illness overtook her, she made it her business to return to the hospital thereby shielding her loved ones from being witness to her devastation.

She put other's needs before her own. She loved us with the innocence of a very young child and at the same time with the protectiveness of a wise and caring adult. There was not one person who ever cared for her, including all the hospital staff, who did not love her for her kindness. Time after time as we met members of the staff at various hospitals, we would have the nurses tell us how special she was.

When she heard of Regina's death, a thirty-five year old nurse who was herself a patient, called to tell me tearfully that Regina had helped her to cope with her depression better than any doctor in the hospital. She credited Regina as being the person truly responsible for helping her to recover. Regina was only seventeen years old at the time of this hospitalization.

For all her personal hurts and sorrows, Regina could never bear to see sadness in anyone that she loved. A tear in your eye would produce one in hers, along with a hug to comfort you. When Bob returned from the hospital after a heart attack, she made sure that he was recovered and comfortable at home before she let us know how badly she needed to get back to the hospital. As father and daughter, they were blessed with an extraordinary empathy and devotion to one another.

When I first realized the seriousness of Regina's illness, I started reading books that I thought would help us in our relationship with her. Most books that dealt with Regina's problems pointed out how the symptoms of the illness often lead to the breakdown of family relationships. Her illness had the opposite effect on our family. People who had not spoken to others for years were reunited, strangers became meaningful friends, people pulled together who would have stayed apart just because they were joined together in sympathy for

Regina's suffering. We learned what compassion really means. We all learned to give of ourselves in ways we had never suspected we possessed.

We learned to laugh in new ways too. Regina loved laughter and giggling and shared hilarious anecdotes with us to accomplish this end. She would laugh at her illness and its symptoms. She would poke fun at hospital rules, menus, routines, etc. She would fill us in on her latest crush who was frequently one of the male attendants. If her latest hero's interest was baseball she suddenly became a fan. She exhibited so much humor that most people that knew her in a casual ways could not believe that she really was mentally ill at all.

Yet, the burden of mental illness had caused her to seek her own end at several points during her adolescence and young adulthood. Her father and I, however, feel that God had a special purpose for Regina and would not take her to Himself at those times. God, in his mercy for all those who already loved her, and for those He set in her path to be touched by her special qualities, let her live on to complete His purpose for her in this world. She taught us the true meaning of His message of love for others. She led us, through her painful trials, closer to Him, and now finally to the anticipation of the eternal home He has prepared for us to all share together. Regina Theresa was truly a special child of God."

We played Cindy's song at the close of the minister's message. Its message of welcome to Regina when we were reunited in 1988 was now totally appropriate as a farewell. Everyone there, including the minister, thought it had just been composed solely for the memorial. Although most everyone was crying while it was played, I was totally at peace, smiling to myself, filled with God's love and with assurance that Regina was with Him.

It turned out to be a beautiful service in spite of the snow and the delay. I was thankful to God for His message to me through Regina's last telephone call, "Dad, I only called to tell you I went to church today." I recognized that Regina's suicide attempt was allowed to succeed this time because she had cried out to Him for help. She had turned her life over to Him and asked Him to take her. In His mercy for this severely disturbed child and her life of turmoil, He lifted her to Himself and embraced her as His lost child returned home. Gloria and I know that this is true. God miraculously revealed many things to us through Regina's death that led us to the knowledge that the Lord allowed Regina to die in a state of grace.

Also, Richie had given us tremendous peace of mind when he told us about Regina's appearance when he went to visit her body before she was cremated. He said that she looked like she was quietly sleeping. There were no signs of facial discoloration or bruises on her neck. He said that her facial expression was happy.

### Gloria's comments

*What a remarkable week we had following Regina's passing. Love and compassion flowed like a river. God gave me phenomenal strength and insight.*

*On Wednesday I had started to feel guilty about the quality of love I had given Regina. God did not want me feeling that way for long. He just wanted me to experience my own guilt so that I would be prepared to speak to the kids in the family later that day. So, within a short time after my self-blaming thoughts started, He had me suddenly find a card that Regina had given to me several years earlier which stated how perfectly I had helped to cheer up her life. I had forgotten the card ever existed. The greeting said:*

"You're Someone Very Special to Me

It's nice to be needed,
And I just thought I'd tell you
How much I need a person like you in my life.
I really count on your way
Of knowing what I'm trying to say
When I have trouble finding the words.
You restore my faith
In good things and good people.
You teach me to enjoy
The bright spots in each new day,
You help me smile
When I might have shed a tear
Please don't ever change
I need you
And appreciate you so much
For the person you are............"

*Nothing could have lifted my spirits more than this card signed by Regina. Did an angel hide it last August and come back to have it surface on this one day in time? It wouldn't have surprised me one bit if this were so.*

*When I showed the card to everyone around the table that night, Cindy remarked, "has anyone noticed the hand on the front of the card?" The picture showed a chocolate colored hand holding a red rose. It was so typical of Regina, not to see that the card was designed* for a black family. Regina never noticed the color of a person's skin. She looked straight inside to find goodness and love.

I remembered the card and its image of a hand holding a rose all during the week. It brought me comfort. I did not realize how important it would become to me the following week, when I would be caught in a spasm of renewed guilt. I did not foresee that God had another of his miraculous God-incidences in store for me.

When my nieces and nephews came Wednesday night, they found me upstairs in Cindy's room just beginning a conversation concerning suffering. All four wandered in one by one, sat down on the bed and floor, and started to ask tearful questions. Patrick joined them. One by one they confessed how they felt, relating incidents which condemned their own behavior and asking many questions, questions that God had already given me answers for. I did not have to stop and think. I was completely in the hands of the Holy Spirit. Healing words flowed from me to these youngsters. Cindy, who had turned her life over to the Lord when she was fifteen, later reported that she watched in awe as the power of the Holy Spirit seemed to radiate from me.

The message I delivered was simple. Regina was to have many rewards in heaven. Her life of suffering here on earth was short but purposeful. We all had a reason to feel guilty, but we were to use that guilt to teach us to love others as Regina loved us in spite of our flaws. She understood our repugnance toward some of the events of her life. She did not expect us to make up for her wounds. She was here to show us something of the purity of God's love in the midst of sin. She was here to teach us *about loving one another.*

*I told them that her recent surrender to God was rewarded by His deliverance from the bondage of her disease, allowing her to leave all suffering behind. What appeared to be a tragedy was in fact a blessing.*

*I told the children they should no longer feel guilty, but that they should use their memories to remind themselves to be kind to people they might otherwise ignore and to be charitable to strangers, who like Regina, might have become homeless and destitute due to mental illness.*

*Regina's memorial service was only two days away, and I had no idea of appropriate dress for the occasion. When I consulted with Bob's ex-wife, she told me to dress informally and wear whatever Regina was used to seeing us in. I thought this was a touching idea, so our whole family dressed informally. I wore a white sweater that Regina had given to me on Mother's Day and a pair of slacks. I guess Regina was used to seeing her mother dressed in business clothes, because when Ann showed up she was wearing a dark suit, with high heels.*

*I suddenly felt ashamed of my outfit. When I was introduced to the minister, I apologized for my white sweater and explained that Regina had given it to me. The Pastor replied that my sweater was perfectly appropriate, since white is the color of resurrection.*

*As part of the memorial service, the minister read in its entirety, a letter from Valerie, that revealed Bob's love and concern for all his children, particularly for Regina in her illness. Valerie had faxed her impressions to the Pastor, at his request, to help in the composition of the sermon he would give. She never expected it to be read from the pulpit. It was a beautifully written testimony of a man's deep love for his special child. It highlighted their unique relationship:*

"Dear Pastor Meyer,

I was very happy to hear that you would be leading the memorial service for Regina this Saturday.

I am aware that it will probably be difficult for you to reflect upon aspects of Regina's life past her early childhood since we were not in close contact with you during recent years. Perhaps I can share some of my thoughts with you in the hope that it will give you a clearer picture of the person she grew to become.

Regina, from the time that she was a small child, felt both the joys and sorrows that we encounter in life, at a level much deeper than many people, even depth of those of us who grow to be mature, sensitive, experienced adults. This may have caused many things to be more burdensome for Regina, but it also allowed her to see positive and wonderful things in people she that came in contact with. She had an incredible ability to see beyond a person's outer appearance, social class or other aspects that so many of us use to judge our fellow human beings. She showed kindness to everyone, regardless of who they were or what they may have done and gave the rest of us a beautiful example to follow in terms of loving one another without judging one another.

Regina's most important relationship was the one that she shared with our father, Robert Mascarelli. About five years ago, when we first came back into contact with my father and his side of the family, Regina was leading the way step by step. With all the turmoil that had occurred in our family over the years, we were welcomed with open arms by a loving group of aunts, uncles, cousins, grandparents, and of course, our father and step-mother Gloria Mascarelli.

Like Patrick and myself, Regina never felt so much love and support from so many people. Everyone who came in contact with Regina recognized the warm, sweet giving person that she was and she always responded with love.

Regina, as I previously said, was extremely close to my father and step-mother. She felt accepted and cared for and the love that was exchanged between them was a kind of love that cannot easily be described in words. The emotion that was felt between the three of them and the willingness for self-sacrifice and compassion that was an everyday part of their relationships went so far beyond even the strongest parent-child relationships.

In particular, our father stood by Regina every step of the way. When the rest of the family would have moments of emotional exhaustion from Regina's illness, when we would lose patience, or become resentful of the "inconvenience" that came along with Regina's situation, he remained steadfast in his love for her. It was always he who had the words of encouragement for Regina or who was never, for a second, reluctant to offer whatever support that she needed. He is exceptional, with a heart of gold, a loving and generous man whose best qualities Regina also shared.

The reason I am concentrating on Regina's relationship with my dad is because I realize that you were not witness to many things that happened in the past few years. I know that it would be Regina's wish that our father be recognized at her memorial. He meant a great deal to her and he still means a lot to Patrick and me. Despite the temporary estrangement from him that we experienced as children,

our parents are of equal importance to us, and
Patrick and I both wish that this be expressed at
this service on Saturday.
I know that Gloria is sending you some further
notes regarding the family and Regina's role in our
lives so I won't keep writing much longer. I could
probably do this all day long!
Thank you again for the love and support that you
have shown my family.

Love always,<br>Valerie"

*At last my husband was vindicated from the accusa-
tions of being a bad father that his children's stepfather
had used to separate the children from Bob. Ann's
friends, who had heard the lies and perhaps believed
them, were there at the funeral home to hear about the
deep love and concern Bob had for his children through
a letter that was written by his oldest child and presented by a man of God in a public place.*

*I know for sure that Bob, in his genuine humility,
did not even notice his ultimate victory over the lies of
the past. However, my children and I, Valerie, Patrick
and Regina herself (if God allows such things), were
more than happy to see the truth revealed to all the
people in that room. Again, God was using Regina's love
for us to heal our past hurts as we had prayed to heal
hers.*

# Chapter 13

## Signs and Wonders

Bob's journal continued
March 19, 1993

My ex in-laws left on Monday, the 16th, the day after the memorial service. Richie left on Tuesday. Patrick was with his mother at their apartment. Wednesday the 18th, we took Valerie to the airport so she could return to her husband and two children in Canada.

I decided we should have lunch with Cindy, Patrick and my ex-wife on the way. My relationship with Ann had been often strained, even after we met at the hospital conference, but Regina's death had left us united in our sense of loss. We'd decided to get together at a restaurant on our way to the airport, so that Valerie could have some extra time with her mother before she left.

As sometimes happens, the waitress keyed into our conversation regarding the funeral and asked which of the two women was Regina's mother. Gloria responded that Ann was, but Ann answered, "both of us were her mother." Gloria was very touched by this acknowledgment. I was, frankly, very surprised. As we stood to leave Ann turned to me with a kiss and stated, "We lost our daughter." God sure had been busy healing hearts that week. This has been a remarkable time. I would never have thought I could bear surviving the death of my special girl. Only God could have turned my suffering into victory.

That afternoon would be the first time Gloria and I would be alone in our house since before we got the news of Regina's death. I was anxious to get back home because the feeling of Regina's presence was so strong there. I'd received so many God-given messages of comfort that week. I felt there would be some additional comfort waiting for me and that somehow I would receive a personal message from Regina after everyone was gone.

Without revealing this intuitive hunch to Gloria, I started to do a casual inspection of the house, walking through all the rooms and looking for some sign from Regina that would have some special meaning to me. I noticed the butterfly drawing was still posted on the refrigerator door, but nothing else seemed unusual.

I walked into Regina's room and sat on her bed. I was surrounded by all the possessions she treasured enough to leave with us instead of chancing their loss at a hospital. She'd hung trinkets from threads attached to the ceiling. The wall next to her bed was covered with photos of family and friends. Letters were also posted there, many from the staff of hospitals that she had been in. The closet was filled with the clothes she would rush out to buy when her social security checks came in.

Up in the corner of the room was the inflated balloon with a plush rabbit inside that I had given to Regina last Easter. The shelves of her bookcase were filled with gifts and souvenirs. There were plastic bags of institutional soap that Regina had collected. We knew that one would accompany her back from each of her hospital placements.

The room was filled with her personality. I felt very close to her. Gloria was very wise in disobeying my emotionally charged order to discard all of Regina's things. I felt Regina's presence in the room, but I did not receive any special message at all. I remembered that Gloria and Cindy had spent hours going through all of Regina's papers looking for anything that would explain her sudden suicide. She had only visited us several months ago, and we had no indication that her mental status had changed in any way.

After finding nothing special, I decided to go back downstairs and rejoin Gloria. It was about six p.m. and Gloria was deeply involved in conversation with Cheryl on the phone. Cheryl had cried throughout the funeral service. She'd come with her intended husband who had known Regina only briefly.

Cheryl had stayed away from our house during the week following Regina's death. She was so upset that she preferred to remain alone to sort out her reaction. She stayed at her apartment and didn't fully share in the loving experiences that were taking place in our home. Gloria spoke to her every day, however, filling her in on all the positive details of significance that had lifted our spirits during the week.

Gloria hung up the phone and prepared a snack for us. We then watched Regina's lip-synching video that was given to us by a family friend who had Regina stay at her house on a recent occasion. Regina loved to pretend that she could sing and play the guitar, and that is how she presented herself in her home video. We both were happy that we would have this recent tape of her to keep forever.

Later, at about eight p.m., Gloria came back from the upstairs bedrooms crying. Without telling me, she too had gone to Regina's room. I will ask her to report what happened in her own words when she gets to read this journal and writes this chapter of our book.

### Gloria's comments

*When I entered Regina's room after watching the video, I sat on her bed and just let my mind wander for a bit. Richie had used this room when he was here. I remembered cleaning the room and changing the sheets just before he arrived. I'd moved a suitcase into the corner, where I now noticed it for the first time since he'd gone. It suddenly occurred to me that I did not know what was in it. Regina left it behind several months ago after her last visit. As I bent over to unzip the top, my heart started to race. Cindy and I had not searched this bag.*

*I didn't know exactly what I was looking for, but I had a hunch that there was something in the bag that I must find. At first glance, I saw nothing but clothing. I felt disappointed. "Lord", I thought, "I feel there is some kind of message here. Where is it?"*

As I searched through the contents a second time, I saw a small magazine laying between the clothes. It was the same kind of word search puzzle book that Bob was accustomed to using when he was bored at antique shows. Since Regina had returned from New Orleans by bus this last time, I concluded that she'd bought it to pass the time on the long trip. Ordinarily, I would not have even glanced at the book. This type of puzzle is a no-brainer, and I am a crossword puzzle snob. But, since I was going to give it to Bob, I sifted through the pages to see how many puzzles were left undone. Regina had not used the book at all. Perhaps she had planned to give it to her Dad as a gift. Then I noticed a that a piece of paper had been slipped inside the pages.

On a lined piece of loose-leaf paper was a note written on November 23, 1992. Regina had written it as her own obituary prior to her anticipated suicide.

"Oh, my God," I thought, "this is what I have been looking for all week. Why did it take so long to find?"

My mind was spinning with nervous anticipation as I read each line. Regina dispassionately presented her name and birthday with an open date for her death in 1993. She was not sure which method she would use to commit suicide. She stated that she did not want to go on living and that her family would be "pleased with her decision." She ended with a plea to God. "Please take me" she had written.

Had she made the same plea the Sunday she went to church, one day before her suicide? Of course she did, I reasoned. God had received her prayers and granted her wish. I had already been assured by the Lord that Regina had died in grace. I knew that from the moment I saw her butterfly picture. I had already told the whole family about my revelation, but what was this statement about her family being happy with her decision? She must have thought that we would be relieved to be rid of her.

"Oh, dear Lord" I thought as I reviewed this line over and over again, "did Regina commit suicide because she felt we were better off without her?"

All of a sudden the guilt that I'd felt when I contemplated her death several weeks earlier came back to me with Satanic fury. It was my fault that Regina had died. She thought I was tired of caring for her. She left this world to rid us of her burden. These thoughts immediately robbed me of all the peace I had achieved during the preceding week.

When I remembered the card with the hand holding the rose, I was not soothed by its message that she was helped by the love and attention I had given her. I remembered suddenly that she had called me to say she had especially picked out this card for me. Surely , that message must be important, I reasoned in panic. Why else would the Lord have left it for me to find this week?

"But, no," my guilty conscience responded, "that was how Regina felt then. You changed your feelings for her with the increasing burden of her illness, and she knew you were tired of all her problems. She died because she thought you didn't care for her anymore. Why else would she write that her family would be happy with her decision?"

The oppression of these thoughts was too heavy for me to bear alone. With an ache in my chest and fear of my husband's hurt response to this unusual message, I went downstairs with the letter to read it to Bob. It was *perfectly natural for me to read it to him rather than hand it to him. Bob was not able to decipher her hand-writing. I could not stop crying.*

Bob's journal continued

Gloria found a letter inserted in a word search puzzle book. Regina knew I was the only one who would be interested in the book, so she must have meant her message for me. Gloria called out, "I have something for you from Regina" as she came down the stairs. "Oh good," I responded as I turned off the television set. Gloria sat beside me to read the letter. My only thought was that I was about to hear the message I had been expecting all day. I had given up all hope this afternoon, suspecting that my intuition was just wishful thinking.

Gloria was trying to read the letter quickly. She was crying. As she was about half way through, she paused and asked me about a loud continuous noise outside the house. She was having difficulty trying to talk over it. "What is that noise?" she asked.

I was more than aware of it; I was in awe of it. It was like the deep rumbling that accompanies an earthquake. One of my arms was slung over the back of the sofa and I could feel the walls of our house vibrate as Gloria was reading to me. My answer to her was, "I don't know and I don't want to know, just finish reading the letter." By the time she read the last word the noise and vibration were gone. I then told Gloria that I had been expecting a message from Regina all day.

God had certainly made me pay attention to Regina's words, especially her prayer for release. He'd arranged a private little earthquake for me to mark the occasion, just another little miracle to complete our extraordinary week and to clarify my thoughts on God's will in all that had happened.

I'd wondered when God would give me an answer about why Regina had not been healed here on earth. I now fully understand why she went to church the day before she died and why she had called to tell me that she'd gone. It was not just my prayers that God was answering. Regina and I were both asking Him for the same thing. Our prayers differed only in that she did not want to remain here on earth. She asked Him to take her to Himself. That was exactly what she prayed for. "Please take me,"she had asked. "Please heal her," I prayed. By answering her prayer, He answered mine as well.

I was feeling so blessed by God and the unseen presence who arranged to have her letter found that day. The knowledge that Regina was with Him, that He had "taken" her as she had asked, filled me with joy. But, I could not explain any of this to Gloria. How could she possibly understand that the Lord had delivered a joyful message to me through Regina's suicide note? Her reaction was so different from mine. The best I could do was to explain.to her that Regina's message brought me some additional comfort.

Gloria, on the other hand, was weeping. She told me about the pain she was feeling inside her chest. She revealed her feelings of guilt. I could not understand her interpretation. Everything in Regina's letter indicated that she was now with the Lord. I was thrilled that the Lord cared so much about me. He was going to a lot of trouble to let me know that Regina was with Him.

I decided that we should go to visit our friends Russ and Janet, Regina's godparents, to tell them about what had just happened. I anticipated that Gloria would feel better if we got out of the house for a while. Besides, I couldn't wait to tell everyone about what had happened. I knew I could count on Gloria to interpret the story as another one of God's miracles. Of course, I would allow her to do all the talking for me, while I sat back with a skeptical expression, making "oo wee" sounds from the Twilight Zone to accompany her tale. It was not yet time to reveal my faith to anyone.

As we opened the door to leave, we were both struck by the vision before us. Silently, it had snowed. The entire landscape was pure white. There were no traffic sounds at all. In the stillness the sense of peace was awesome. Long icicles hung from tree branches and glistened in the light of the street lamps. The solid carpet of white snow gleamed like sequins and lit up the dark night. It was an unforgettable scene. Everything in sight was white. White like the color of the sweater that Regina had given Gloria. White like the color of resurrection. All that was missing was the sound of trumpets descending from Heaven. It was a scene straight out of the Master Artist's imagination.

When we arrived at our friends' house, I was surprised to see that it had not snowed there, even though they lived only eight miles away from us. Was the snowfall a miracle arranged just for us as well?

The next day I examined all the local papers. I called the weather channels and asked my neighbors if they had heard any noises or felt any vibrations the night before. Apparently, nothing unusual had happened to anyone else, except for a quiet neighborhood snowfall that melted in the sunshine the next morning.

## Gloria's comments

*I heard the noise and felt the vibrations, but all I could focus on was the poignancy of Regina's letter. It seemed strange to me that Bob did not share my reaction. He was happy with Regina's message. But, then again, I reasoned,he had nothing to feel guilty about. The pangs of guilt were shifting around in my chest and causing me to feel physical pain. My stomach began to hurt as well. I was relieved to leave the house as Bob suggested.*

*I knew that the sight that greeted us as we opened the door was extraordinary. This was the second snowfall we'd experienced in March, and the last one was on the day scheduled for the memorial service. I knew everything that had happened that week had been miraculous. Yet, I had lost the peace that God had given me, and I could not imagine how I would regain it again. How could I ever be sure that I had not played a role in Regina's desire to commit suicide? Bob had his reassurance granted in such a tangible way. Why, the earth had actually shook for him! Could God possibly forgive me enough to reassure me again? I left the house in pain, returned in pain, slept fitfully and woke up feeling miserable.*

*Bob was whistling while he was shaving the next morning. The sound of his cheer offended me. I felt lost. I wanted to talk to Regina one last time. I wanted to tell her that I loved her. I did not want her to die thinking I*

*had abandoned her. Why did she think I would be
pleased with her decision to die? Where was my comfort
now, Lord?*

*While Bob was shaving and I was feeling abandoned
in my guilt, I walked past Regina's and Cindy's bedrooms and entered the doorway of the room Cheryl had
used when she returned home to live with us. She did
not stay with us long before she moved out on her own
again, taking everything but her TV set with her. As my
eyes wandered around what I thought to be an otherwise empty room, I noticed my small table in the corner.
On this table was an object which would impact my life
from that day forward. Strangely it was the only thing
other than her television set that Cheryl had left behind
when she moved.*

*On the table in the far corner I saw the window
reflected in the glass dome top of the music box that she
had left behind. I knew Cheryl had owned it. I knew it
was a music box. I had forgotten it was still in the room.
I had never taken note of what was in the dome.*

*As I walked closer to look into the glass, my mouth
dropped open in astonishment. I knew immediately that
this object was meant to be left in the house just for me. I
knew at once that God was delivering a unique personal
message of love and forgiveness. Inside the glass dome
of the music box was a porcelain hand holding a rose.
Perched on top of the rose, was a beautiful butterfly!*

*Never in my life was I so completely astonished by
God's power. For He had seen fit to place something in
my home years ago–an object containing the perfect
symbols to console me and pardon me from what could
have been damaging irrational guilt on this particular*

*day. His timing was absolutely perfect. A hand holding a rose, the symbols of Regina's confirmation of her love for me found in her Mother's Day card. A butterfly, representing the drawing that she had prepared for me that had come to signify that she now was with the Lord. There they were, both joined together under the dome of the music box, just waiting for my discovery on that specific morning.*

*God had guided my steps to enter a room I had not tended since Cheryl left. It was, and still is, amazing that both of the symbols which comforted me during the week following Regina's death were found together in one object. A merciful Lord had arranged for my comfort long before, knowing how much I would need His absolution from guilt on that day.*

*God displayed unbounded love by preparing a means of comfort for Bob and for me through the trial of our loss and grief. How generous He was with His gift of discernment to allow us to interpret the signs that revealed our child's victory over suicidal death. God's love lifted us above potential bitterness and heartache and filled us with peace and awe derived from His display of miracles. How great, how great is God's love!*

*Through this very personal experience, the pain of my grief when I discovered the suicide note was lifted forever. I still carry the sadness of missing Regina, especially as I write this, but the raging fire of my guilt was extinguished by the discovery of the music box. It was replaced, instead, with a deep conviction that God's direction for His believers' lives is already in place, just waiting for our discovery.*

*I left Cheryl's room with the music box clutched to*

*my body as Bob, who was walking towards me, heard me say, "You got your message from God last night, but I got mine this morning." My eyes were shining with God's reflected love, overflowing in grateful tears for His merciful attention to my needs. I was quite sure I saw Bob's eyes mist over as well when he looked inside the glass dome. He knew what its symbols meant as well as I did.*

*I called Cheryl immediately to ask her why she'd left the music box behind when she moved out. Her answer was that she didn't know why. She had wanted to throw it out several times but decided to leave it behind instead. But, I already knew the answer. God had planned to have it left just for me.*

Bob's journal continued

When we listened to the melody as we watched the hand holding the rose and butterfly turn, Gloria told me that she'd expected to hear a romantic tune because of the pretty theme. I wasn't at all surprised to hear the music from "It's a Small World After All." The tune wasn't inappropriate at all. We'd sent a musical clown to Regina that played the small world theme just a year before. Coincidences that fit together to complete the picture of God's involvement in our lives were getting to be routine in our house. It was as if God was solving a great puzzle for us, giving us clues whenever we needed them.

## Gloria's comments

*As I was typing these last words from Bob's journal, it occurred to me, now four years later, that I finally understand the passage that was given to Richie by the stranger on the day after Regina's death. It was:*

"Understanding is a wellspring of life unto him
that hath it: but the instruction of fools is folly"

*In giving us the understanding, knowledge and discernment received through faith, we have recognized God's messages that have been made apparent to us by the Holy Spirit. Thus being replenished and refreshed by drinking of the wellspring, we have been able to go on with our lives in comfort and peace of mind. The words "wellspring of life" also refer to everlasting life in eternity, the place where Regina had been received. The second part of the proverb must apply to those who have denied God, fools, who cannot be instructed regarding God because they are spiritually blind. Fools are those who have chosen not to accept God's gift of faith and receive the Holy Spirit. Fools cannot discern God's personal miracles which enable believers to understand God's will and to feel peace in the midst of earthly trials.*

*We do not feel that we were singled out for the appearance of reassuring miracles after the death of a loved one. Many believers who have lost relatives have had similar experiences. To those who have not, they should be comforted through what we have experienced and can now share. We hope our experiences will bless others. As Jesus is quoted in the book of John:*

" ..Blessed are they that have not seen, and yet have
believed."(John 20:29)

# Chapter 14

## The 700 Club Miracle

Bob's journal continued
April 13, 1993

I was watching Pat Robinson's 700 Club TV show this morning. The guest was Lori R., a young girl of Regina's age who was giving her testimony. She spoke of a history of sexual abuse, low self-esteem, prostitution and psychiatric care. Although her problems were not as intense, the similarity of her situation to Regina's life was evident. This young lady had survived her misfortune. She was going on to college and hoped to have a career that would help other unfortunate children.

I began to feel upset, thinking that these were the choices Regina would have made if her life had gone differently. Feeling depressed, I shut off the TV and started to walk to the door, planning to get myself some coffee at a local restaurant. As l left the room I heard the television set go back on.

"Well," I thought, "I'd better go back and watch the program. There might be something I'm meant to hear." I was getting used to looking for messages from the supernatural.

I sat down again to watch the show. A minute or two later, I heard something crash to the floor. I thought that Gloria had gotten out of bed and dropped something. I went upstairs to check, but she was still asleep. I looked into the laundry room. Sometimes my neighbor's cat would wander inside if the door was left open. There was nothing out of place. The kitchen revealed nothing out of the ordinary either. As I walked into the dinning room, I found the photo that we had prepared for Regina's memorial on the floor. It was in a Plexiglas frame so it hadn't broken.

Below the window is a wide ledge that is built up from the floor to a height of about 12 inches. The ledge is covered with thick carpeting. Below where the picture had stood was a large glass bowl set on a brass pedestal. As the picture fell it missed hitting the glass bowl and landed three feet from where it had been.

The frame is a ten by fourteen square of Plexiglas with one inch depth all around into which a fitted cardboard box is placed. To hold a picture, the cardboard box has to be removed, the photo inserted with its face to the clear front, and the cardboard box reinserted to hold it in place. The cardboard has a tab that can be pulled out for hanging, but we had decided to place the picture on the window sill, leaning its back on the window. Because the front is Plexiglas and the back just cardboard, the frame's weight is all on the picture side.

This frontal weight would lend itself to toppling over, so the fact that it fell off the ledge is not that remarkable. What is strange, is that the picture fell past the carpeted ledge, traveled a distance and landed on the floor <u>face up</u>.

The other thing that is surprising is that it landed with a loud noise at the only time I felt despondent since God let me know He had healed Regina by taking her to be with Him. I should have been out of the house having my coffee in the restaurant trying to rationalize my renewed heartache. The television turning itself on again should not have happened at all.

When I found the photo laying there, I saw Regina's face smiling up at me as if to say, "Dad, stop worrying about what might have been. I'm fine. Jesus is taking care of me. See how happy I am now."

When I told Gloria the events that had happened, carefully omitting my own interpretation, she immediately got excited and started to speak of the event as another of the ongoing miracles that had happened since Regina had died.

We were in our car going to visit my parents when I told her the details. All through our car ride and on the way back home, she prodded me with questions about how and where the picture was placed when I found it. As soon as we walked in our door she asked me to place the picture in the exact position I had seen it on the floor.

At her insistence we repeatedly tried to prod the picture to fall from the sill and land somewhere on the floor face up. After many trials and failures, Gloria proved to me that the incident could not be repeated without the picture falling face down. Most times it never made it off the ledge at all. We almost broke our glass bowl trying to get it to fall in the same position that I'd found it.

"There is no reasonable explanation", I said.

"Of course, there is," she replied. "It must have been an angel."

To myself I said silently, "I knew it all the time."

## Gloria's comments

*Later that day, I considered how I could convince Bob that an angelic intervention had taken place in our house and that the events could not be attributed to chance or coincidence. I prepared series of questions to present to him, questions that were geared towards revealing the event as a miracle.*

*Question one: Why was Bob watching the 700 Club, an evangelical program dedicated to spreading God's word? As far as I knew he watched it at night, only when I insisted. He had never seen the show in the morning before. Why hadn't he turned to another station? He usually watched the news.*

*Question two: Why was this particular interview starting when he turned on the TV set? Bob could easily identify the similarities of problems and lifestyle that were presented by the guest, a girl who was the same age and had a similar background to his own daughter.*

*Question three: Why did the TV set go back on spontaneously after he had shut it? That was certainly an unusual event. It had not happened before.*

*Question four: Why did Regina's picture fall at that mo-*

*ment in time, with a crashing sound that required investigation?*

*Question five: How did it land at such a distance from its original position, overcoming obstacles in its way and defying gravity by landing face up?*

*Later, I posed these questions to Bob and explained that any one of these instances occurring independently could be attributed to chance or coincidence, but the combination of all of them happening at once defies logic as well as the laws of physics. The whole series of events seemed directed towards Bob's discovery of Regina's picture smiling up at him from the floor. No human hand had caused it to fall. I restated my original conclusion; it must have been an angel.*

*This time Bob did not deny the possibility of a miracle. Although he did not enthusiastically agree with me, he showed no reluctance to my idea of joining the 700 Club. We have been members ever since, often listening to other accounts of miracles that have been linked to this powerful television ministry.*

*Bob did not record the two other "happenings" that occurred during those first healing weeks after Regina's death. The first involved Bob's daughter Valerie as she sat at our kitchen table several days before the memorial service.*

*When Regina was a resident at the state hospital for children she had made a small heart shaped wooden plaque attached to a spring loaded clothes pin. It was painted pink and had the word "Mom" hand written by Regina on a smaller white plaque that was glued onto the larger one. I'd clipped it to the handle of a radio that I kept on a high shelf just to the left of the kitchen table.*

*As Valerie sat talking to Patrick, the heart plaque suddenly popped off the radio and landed on the table in front of her. Valerie experienced this incident again during the week. It seemed apparent to me that Bob's children and I were receiving the same message. It was Regina's wish that they would both regard me as a second mom, and that I would open my heart to them with the same love I had for my biological children.*

*The second unusual incident involved our friends, Russ and Janet. They had a large white butterfly suddenly appear in their restaurant kitchen on the following week. It was still March and unusually cold, certainly not the time of year for a butterfly to emerge. They watched it in wonder as it flitted around the kitchen, followed it as it disappeared into another room, and wondered where it had gone.*

*Our friends knew about the significance of the butterfly as a symbol of resurrection and how it had appeared repeatedly in our lives following Regina's death. They had no doubt that they were also receiving a message of Regina's ascension to heaven as an angelic answer to their own personal grief over the loss of their godchild. They felt extraordinarily blessed by the unusual appearance of the white butterfly in their kitchen.*

Bob's journal continued
April 16, 1993

Everything is going well. God's comfort continues in my life. I'm happy that Regina is with Him. It's so nice to know that when I go to bed at night I can fall right to sleep; no bad thoughts, only good. I'm asleep within five minutes. I am still hoping God will give us just a little token money from Nic Stics so I can use it to serve His purpose.

## Gloria's comments

*Although I knew that Bob was reconciled with Regina's death, not once did he openly acknowledge to me that his comfort came from the Lord. He listened to all I had said about our miracles and he even repeated what had happened to our friends and relatives. He was still keeping his personal relationship with God to himself. I sensed his belief rather than knew it for a fact.*

*I was so overjoyed at the concrete evidence of God's intervention to soothe our pain, I repeated events over and over again hoping for Bob to acknowledge them as God's revelation to us. Bob seemed content to let me serve as interpreter of the supernatural. He never denied believing what I said. He was even enthusiastic when I shared the discoveries that the Holy Spirit was giving to me. He was more than happy with the evidence of God's wondrous acts, but where was his praise for the Giver?*

## Gloria's comments continued
Saturday April 18, 1993

*Sometime during those first weeks following Regina's passing, I was talking to Cindy's Greek girlfriend, relating some of the wondrous events that had taken place. She told me that she wasn't surprised since the Greeks believe that the presence of the departed remains on earth for forty days following their death.*

*This seemed entirely reasonable to me at the time since we all felt Regina was still close to us. I made a point of marking the fortieth day on my calendar, with hopes that we would still receive some special messages before that time. I remember feeling that I might be acting superstitious by thinking this way, and I prayed to God to forgive me if I was.*

*I stopped thinking about all this and got caught up in daily events. But, I did remember the fortieth day nonetheless. On that morning, Bob left the house to visit a friend and I went up to Regina's room to sit on her bed and wait for something to happen. Nothing did. After about a half hour of quiet, I started to look through her drawers again, hoping to find something that she left which I might have missed. I was praying off and on for just one more thing that the Lord might give me that would rekindle the wonder of His involvement with us. I found nothing. I sat down on the bed again and let my mind wander. "Just one more thing, Lord, please just one more thing," I kept thinking. More time passed without anything eventful happening.*

*I told myself that I had been superstitious. Beyond that, I was being selfish. After all that had been done for me, what right did I have to ask God for another of His amazing signs? The music box was downstairs on the bookcase in the den where I could see it every day. That was all that I would ever need to remind me of His miracles. I was acting stupidly just sitting there when I had so many other things to do around the house. How arrogant of me to ask God for anything more! He had given me so much already. Was I getting so "high" on His interventions that I needed another fix to keep me*

*going? How ungrateful could I be? "Forgive me, Lord,"
I thought as I got off the bed and walked to the doorway.*

*Just before I left the room I noticed the white balloon
hanging in the corner. "Of course," I thought, "this is the
balloon that Bob gave to Regina last Easter a little over a
year ago". It was the only Easter that she had spent with
her father since she was a child. What really made it
special was that Valerie had come from Canada to spend
the holiday with us also, and Bob gave them both large
helium filled balloons that had plush rabbits inside
them.*

*I remembered that we had spent some time trying to
figure out how the animals had been placed inside.
Valerie broke her balloon to bring her rabbit home with
her to Canada, but Regina let hers float to touch the
ceiling in the corner of her room and tacked the string to
the wall. It was like a fixture there, along with about
twenty other objects that she had thumb-tacked to her
ceiling so that they were suspended over her bed.*

*I walked over to see if I could clearly see the animal
that was inside. When I got closer I saw that the balloon
had a design on it, but it was not until I was within a foot
of it that I could see what the design was. White on
white, opaque white on transparent white; the balloon's
pattern was made up of <u>butterflies</u> and <u>roses.</u>*

*Once again my mind soared to commune with the
Holy Spirit. I felt the same perfect rapport that I had
experienced when I discovered the music box. Touched
by the evidence of His personal communication with me,
I felt a momentary sensation of the joy that must prevail
throughout Heaven.*

*I wished that Bob were with me to share in my*

196

*discovery. I could hardly contain my excitement. I did not know at the time that God was giving me all these signs and wonders for a special reason. I did not know then that I was to fulfill the promise that Bob had made to Him; to write the book about prayers and miracles that had been recorded in his journal. Well, what a story God has given me to tell!*

*I can hardly contain the surprise that I feel as I type this section of our account. It seems that I have missed one of the most significant messages that God has given us for all these years.*

*It has never occurred to me that there was no logical way for an inflated balloon, particularly with a stuffed animal inside, to survive in its inflated state for over a year without breaking. I remember that it was only about two weeks after Pentecost that I went back into Regina's room and found the stuffed animal on the floor in the corner. I have no knowledge of the exact day that the balloon broke, because I did not recognize its inflated state as being miraculous at the time.*

*It is only now, as I read Bob's diary and trace the events I recorded on my 1993 calendar, that the significance of the inflated balloon becomes even more important than its symbols of butterflies and roses. Inflated latex balloons do not survive that long under normal conditions. But since when do God's ways have to conform to what we humans think of as normal?*

*God has given me, at this time, new insight into the work of his will regarding the miracle of resurrection. From Easter 1992 to Easter 1993, the balloon remained intact. Forty days after Regina's death, on the day before Orthodox Easter, Pentecost, I discovered its message of* roses and butterflies. Sometime within the next two weeks, the balloon broke leaving the stuffed animal on the floor for me to discover. Now, six years later, I am just beginning to recognize how special the balloon really was. To me it now represents the gift of Easter and acts as another reinforcement of the promise of bodily resurrection that exists for all believers.

# Chapter 15

## The Road to Jerusalem

Bob's journal continued
June 16, 1993

Well it has certainly been quiet around here since you took Regina, Lord. I can't say that it doesn't hurt not to have her around. I was so used to anticipating her calls. Now there are endless days stretched ahead of me without hearing her voice. I know that she's with you in a fantastic place filled with the colors of heavenly jewels and the music of adoration, a place that's too wonderful for me to understand. I also know that she is joyous and happy to be free of all the haunting memories that filled her with such intense self-hatred. I know that just facing each day was a trial for her.

I am very grateful that she is with you Lord. It's just that with all the plans you've made for me, I know that it will be a while before I see her again. Things have not happened in the correct order. I should have been with You first to greet her someday, instead of the other way around. I know that Regina and I were both praying for her healing at the same time, but her prayer requested that she be taken up to You. I wanted her healed in this life.

I can't fathom how You go about answering prayers. Whose do You acknowledge first, and for what reason? Although I wonder at these mysteries, I know that the answers are beyond any human comprehension and that Your ways are not our ways. One thing I am sure of though, Your answers and reasons are justified. You have strengthened my faith to a point of complete trust. My questions are only curiosity, not critical.

I remember when Regina was only five years old; innocent, vivacious, wide-eyed and smiling. Gloria and I had just gotten together and we had all my kids for the weekend. "Grandma" came to see us and Regina volunteered to show Gloria's mom our new home. Regina took her by the hand through each room while talking nonstop, explaining each room's function and where everyone slept. That's how I imagine it will be when I get to heaven. I see Regina as my happy little guide.

I think of all the other times she tried to commit suicide, and You never let it happen. I know now that You waited until she prayed to You before you took her. Thank you, Lord.

My imagination sees her dancing around heaven, giggling in happiness, the way I used to see her here from time to time. Those times were insignificant compared to the times I saw her depressed and silent, or anguished with her haunting voices. So all in all, I know she's in the best of all possible places, being with You. What makes it really hard on me is that I can't tell everyone about all the great miracles You've performed for us; the knowledge You've given us that Regina was meant to leave us now.

Gloria, as usual, has been talking enough for both of us, and I do have the opportunity to lend verbal support to her accounts, but I can't initiate any "miracle" talk because I'm not supposed to acknowledge that I'm a believer until it's revealed to Gloria in my journal.

The journal can't be read by her until we get to Israel.

The book can't be started until she reads the journal.

We can't get to Israel until we make some money from the invention to get us there.

Now Lord, You did get this whole thing started. I know Your timing is supposed to be perfect. You took Regina within the six months to a year that I prayed for her to be healed. The time for Nic Stics is running out. Can I get some kind of hint when I can start looking around for airline tickets?

June 28, 1993

I'm going on the principle that it is correct that "God helps those who help themselves." Armed with a print-out of drug companies (six hundred of them) obtained from my brother's pharmacy, I have started to call each one in hopes of generating some interest in our smoking substitute. I got through about three hundred of them this week and actually got thirty-five interested enough to ask for some printed information on the product. I guess that I should feel encouraged.

July 3, 1993

On Wednesday, we went to New Jersey on an interview with a small drug company. They manufacture over-the-counter medications. I think they will be disappointed to find out that our product is going to need to go through FDA testing before it is approved as a prescription drug. I don't think they are big enough to shoulder that expense. We will see what happens after they get all the information.

August 23, 1993

Gloria, my comedienne, thinks we should paper one of our bathrooms with the rejection letters we have gotten from the drug companies. She says we can hang our patent right in the center of them. She has also enlightened me with the proper epitaph for my gravestone. It should read, "Antique dealer, author, inventor-died broke." I guess she's getting a mite discouraged. Now, I should be discouraged too, but I'm not. If God healed Regina and got our patent approved against all odds, He can certainly get me some money from His idea and get us to Israel.

Actually, these last weeks have been more encouraging in a discouraging sort of way. Ultimately, both budding prospects that have bloomed are suffering from arrested development; one from lack of funds and the other with unsuitability.

The unsuitable one was the first real offer we have had. It came from a company in the Midwest that was anxious to purchase our patent outright. This sounded good enough until I heard the amount. They were offering us a pittance. Our attorney figured out that they wanted our patent in order to facilitate the development of their own invention which contained a possible conflict that had been overlooked by the patent office. We were told not to get involved in the deal because our attorney suspected that our patent would be shelved and that we would never get any royalties at all.These recent offers, even if unacceptable, still give me hope that another will work out soon.

Imagine, Gloria just finished lecturing me about faith and prayer. When she looks at me she must see a stubborn and unyielding man. She is nagging me with her fears about me not being born again. Little does she know how dependent I am on continuous prayer to God. She doesn't know that God developed the idea of Nic Stics. She doesn't know about the diary. But, she sure knows how to nag, even if it's for the worthy cause of my redemption. It's going to be a fantastic life for both of us when she finds out that I have already done all that she has asked.

It will be wonderful, no more nagging!

August 30, 1993

I called a local drug company that seemed very interested in Nic Stics last week and they never returned my call. I called the company that offered to buy our patent to see if they were willing to raise their offer. They were supposed to call us back but haven't. Yet, I believe something good is going to happen soon.

August 31, 1993

At last, today I received a call from the local drug company . Surprise of surprises, it looks like we may have a deal after all. It seems that the delay was due to a vacation interruption and all that now remains to cinch the deal is an agreement on a royalty cap. I am aware that I asked the Lord for a small amount, so I will agree with whatever the drug company offers. After all, it is God's deal not mine.

September 7, 1993
10:00 a.m.

We are supposed to get a contract today. Waiting, waiting, waiting.

4:30 p.m.

The lawyer just called to tell us the contract is in. The details are better than I ever expected. We are to get a $25,000.00 option for six months while the company examines the patent and prepares to petition the FDA. Our royalties will be between five percent and seven percent although we probably will not see any of that money for a few years.

September 16, 1993

The contract is here, sitting on my desk. The prophecy that the Holy Spirit gave to me in May of 1990, has come to pass. There has been a long delay, but I understand the reasons for it now. Everything had to evolve according to God's plan, not mine. The Lord knew that my stubborn nature would require time and circumstance to build my faith. That is probably why He told me to hide my diary and my belief until now. If others had known I might have been influenced by their opinions. Also, I may have been fearful of the ridicule that one member of my family received for her beliefs. I guess the Lord knew my comfort zone and made it easy for me to establish a private relationship with Him. Now that he has prepared me, I am ready to share my faith with Gloria

Even knowing all this it still amazes me that the idea that barely interested the patent attorney, that people thought would never get patented, that had the remotest chance of finding an interested manufacturer, has finally been validated.

God has been generous with me. I didn't have to get anything more than His loving care for Regina. I didn't need anything more than the miracles He sent to heal the wounds I might have forever suffered over her death.

But, God has been faithful to the promise He made me and has provided me with the means to go ahead and take our hoped for trip to Israel. Now it is time to implement God's next plan for our lives. It is time for Gloria to learn all about this journal, my faith in the Lord, and my desire to fulfill my promise to write a book to glorify His name.

Later today, Gloria and I will go to the travel agent to make plans for our trip. She doesn't know about all the wonderful strange happenings that culminated in this trip. I wonder how she will react when she reads this diary in Israel and finds out how God had His hand in everything that has happened to us since I first began to pray. I won't have to wonder for long.

September 21, 1993

I spoke to the drug company this afternoon, and after some wording changes, the contract has been approved and we'll be signing it this Thursday at 4:00 p.m.

September 23, 1993

We just signed our option agreement with the drug company and received a check for $25,000.00. We expect to go on to a full licensing agreement within six months. Right now, however, we are getting ready to leave for Israel next week.

Sept. 27, 1993

In order for our faith to be documented and passed on to our children, it would be advisable for every Christian to keep a diary of prayer requests, so that all things that are given to us by God are recorded. This record would serve as an encouragement to the growth of a strong faith in young lives that have not yet been tested by life's trials.

We will be leaving for Israel in several days and finally I will be in complete fellowship with my special wife. Gloria, when you read this, I hope you will know how much I love you.

## Gloria's Comments

*I had long awaited the revelation of the new project that Bob had planned to tell me about when we got to Israel. I confess, I never really expected to make the trip. I was amazed that a drug company had just handed us a check for $25,000.00, just for the option to examine a patent I never had full confidence in.*

*I went to Israel anticipating a spiritual experience, a vacation from our hectic life, to see relatives whom I'd never expected to meet, and visit the religious sights common to both my Jewish background and Christian tradition. I certainly never thought I'd be given a job within hours of setting foot on Israeli soil.*

*Our plane set down in Tel Aviv in the late afternoon. My first reaction was not to bend down and kiss the earth as so many of my fellow Jews were inspired to do when they first set foot on the soil of their homeland. Instead, I was rapidly pushed along by a tired sweaty crowd, through the airport terminal to our baggage and into the rental auto agency across the street from the airport. Although we had made arrangements for a car at home, the usual irritating last minute changes in model and price had to be dealt with. After an annoying delay, we finally got our luggage into the car and drove the relatively short distance between Tel Aviv and our destination, Jerusalem. We found our way to our chosen hotel in the New City, checked in, had dinner and returned to our room.*

*Bob went straight to his suitcase and removed a bright green cloth attaché case that I had never seen before nor packed when we left New York. As he re-*

*vealed its contents he explained that the items it held were related to the new project that I had been told would be revealed when we got to Israel. I had tried to pry the information from him on the plane, but he had steadfastly refused to share anything with me. The contents of the briefcase were put on the desk. I saw a spiral notebook a tape recorder and some pens.*

*Bob smiled at me and explained that these items were related to his project and that he was going to take a long walk while I read the contents of the notebook. I was to record my comments on the tape recorder as I read and he would return to discuss them with me in a few hours. With no other explanation he turned and walked out the door.*

*Within minutes of entering the tiny hotel room, I was left alone with an assignment that baffled me. I was totally unnerved by Bob's strange behavior and the task ahead of me. It was with curious uneasiness that I turned the cover of the notebook to see the first words, "We are all nobodies"..."Can God talk to us?" It was dated June of 1990.*

*As I quickly fanned the pages I discovered many other dates and entries and I realized that this was a personal diary, written in Bob's script, in which he talked about his relationship with God and and the events of our lives. The last entry was dated September 27, 1993 just days before we began the trip.*

*My astonishment grew with every page I read. The realization that Bob had a clandestine faith and that he had recorded it all in a secret diary was dwarfed by my reaction that Bob had written anything at all. He had written an intimate account of our lives for over three years and I had not had a single clue that it was going on.*

*Bob and the written word have never gotten along.He had barely passed English in High School. He was dyslexic, a disorder that had not been named in the years he was a student. He would never take up a pen to even write a letter. Bob would no more think of writing than giving up his precious cigarettes during those tumultuous years. Yet, write he did—a faithful, many times indecipherable, and definitely ungrammatical account which he was handing over to me to edit and construct into a book.*

*There before me were his written words. Why had he written a diary? Why didn't I know he was searching for God? Little by little the contents of the notebook revealed the depth of faith that my husband had acquired during the years of its writing. I was amazed at the intricacies that were woven by God to capture our attention–how often we were getting similar messages from the Holy Spirit.*

*Instead of feeling elated as Bob had expected, I was dismayed and confused. Who was this man, my husband, anyway? Was he still the happy go lucky carefree guy that kept his deeper emotions hidden? He had certainly done a good job of hiding his feelings from me in the past. Was he the amazing unbelievably optimistic man who survived his daughter's death without residual bitterness or anger? Or, was he the man I read about in his journal, a sensitive skeptic, a seeker of God, a now confirmed believer with unshakable faith, a man ready to broadcast his belief to the world through a book revealing his intimate prayer life? I was going to have to get to know my husband all over again.*

*When Bob returned to the room many hours later with a shy smile on his lips and arms open for a hug from me, he found me dazed by what I had read and confused about the person I was embracing.*

*Our three week trip to Israel was the beginning of a new project just as Bob had predicted, but he did not realize that my project of priority was going to be getting to know him in the person of a believing Christian and not the man I thought I had known.*

*We were together in spirit as we wandered the hills that stretch to the borders of Syria. We stood together in awe viewing the gnarled old Olive tree that has been accepted as the place Jesus rested on the night he was taken captive. We sat together in silence, holding hands on a tired old bench in an open air sanctuary just feet from the sea of Galilee where we felt His Holy Presence. We stood together, really together, at the mound that once held the Cross upon which His earthly body had died.*

*We wandered the Old City, walked where He had walked, watched my beloved Jewish people dance with joy in the square before the Wailing Wall on the night of Simchas Torah. Y'shua Ha Mashiach, Jesus the Savior had re-joined us in common faith in His city. He bonded us anew within the walls of the City upon which the fate of the whole world rests.*

*I will never forget the moment, I rushed to the women's side of the Wailing Wall. I stood there as a Messianic Jew alongside the praying Orthodox Jewish women and stuffed a written prayer asking for the healing of my dear Catholic friend who had cancer. I knew with a surety that she would be healed. She was!*

*We talked about our miracles as we traveled the roads of the Holy Land. Everything that God had planned for us came into sharp focus. We laughed about Bob's assumed role of "devils advocate" which he portrayed in order to cajole his brother to teach him about the Lord. We planned the book that would be written.*

*Our trip was successful in every respect. It was spiritually significant, visually remarkable, a treat of previously unexperienced activities, (particularly our half day camel ride into the hills beyond Elat which stretch into Egypt), and a reintroduction to my husband as a Spirit filled Christian with whom I could now freely fellowship.*

# Chapter 16

## Then to Now

**Gloria's Comments**

*The past six years since Regina's death and our trip to Israel have been the best of our marriage. Our former dissatisfactions with one other have taken a back seat to the new insights that the Lord has given us concerning ourselves. The faith that we now share allows us a new level of communication which helps us avoid the pitfalls of resentment and repressed anger that we experienced earlier in our relationship.*

*We consider ourselves to be sort of free floating, Christ-centered, Bible based believers. In actual terms, that means we do not belong to any one church, but attend many different services. The fact that we have not nested in one particular church or denomination has never been a conscious decision that we have made. We travel and work on weekends in our antique business,* and it is almost impossible to get to church during show hours. When we are at home, we attend a Bible based local church and participate in a weekly bible study group.

We are unhappy about the lack of a firmly established Sabbath. We compensate by trying to acknowledge the Holy Spirit in every aspect of our daily lives, frequently discussing His influence in our decision making and viewpoints. We listen to Christian radio or to Christian music when we travel. We do our best not to get caught up in the snares of temporal living that pulled us away from a steady awareness of God before we accepted Christ as the head of our marriage.

The project of writing this book was begun, shelved, and renewed several times over the next few years as God continued to act in our lives. It was always Bob's priority to get the book out to people, to help them with questions about God and to glorify Him as he had promised in his diary. For me, they were busy hectic years that kept me away from the typewriter.

We sold our house and purchased a new home. Bob's son Patrick frequently used both homes as a revolving door in his efforts to get his life launched as an adult and we found ourselves grappling with his problems, oftentimes eclipsing our own projects in favor of his. Patrick lived with us off and on for three years. The other three children either married or remarried. We became involved in all their plans including all the usual showers and engagement parties. Five new grandchildren quickly entered our lives.

Soon after our Israeli trip in September of 1993, Valerie and her two children came to live with us after her divorce. God had given Bob advance notice of this event as he recorded it in his journal entry of March 29, 1991. She is now happily remarried and has delighted us by adding one of the new grandchildren to our growing family. Cheryl is also married and is now the mother of two. Cindy has just had her second baby; our seventh grandchild.

Our Nic Stics' project did not end up making us wealthy. After examining the patent for a year and a half, the drug company decided to abandon plans for its development. Nevertheless, Bob did get enough money to go to Israel, and get his plans for the book started, just as he had asked of God. As a matter of fact, all of his prayers were answered, except for the ability to finance a television show, which has since been produced by someone else and is currently already popular.

Cindy and Valerie have a singing ministry, becoming a vital part of a praise band at their church. In one way or another, God has answered all of Bob's prayers according to his intent to glorify Him, even though the answer was not always exactly as he expected. His last prayer was for the publication of his book to glorify God, which you, dear reader, now hold in your hand.

God's obvious intervention in our lives has not ceased. He still answers Bob's prayers in very discernible ways. He knows Bob from the inside out and deals with him in ways he cannot ignore. A perfect example of this occurred in early February 1996.

On February 14th, 1996, the day that Cindy was scheduled to deliver her first baby, both she and Sonny, my son-in-law, invited me to come to the hospital to share in the birthing experience. It was the first time I had been in a delivery room since Cindy's birth thirty years earlier, and I was to be her coach. We were all excited with the prospect of seeing the new baby. Cindy was nervous about the delivery and I did my best to keep the labor room cheery between the contractions that heralded the baby's arrival. The mood was festive. The induced labor lasted ten hours. Finally, we were all cheering Cindy on, the doctor, nurse, Sonny and myself sounding like a crowd at a football game urging on the winning goal. As little Vincent entered the world, perfectly formed and alert, I was thrilled to be part of the wonderful miracle of birth. I could not wait to share the news with Bob.

I called Bob at three a.m. on February 15th and told him to come to the hospital to greet his new grandson. Bob sounded tired but I insisted that he make the forty-five minute drive to join the celebration. He had done the same for Cheryl when she delivered Joshua in the early morning hours just eleven months earlier. Little Vincent was brought to the window of the nursery for Bob, Cheryl, Valerie and my ex-husband to see, his eyes wide open, looking at us as if he understood we were admiring him. I was filled with the excitement of the birth and was wide awake. Bob was happy but very tired so we started out for home in the separate cars we had taken.

We took a short nap after getting home at about 6 a.m., and then got busy preparing Cindy's apartment for her homecoming the next day. Cindy and Sonny were living in the downstairs apartment of our new house, chosen by us so that we would have a rental income if we needed it. We had not anticipated that they would *want to live this far east on Long Island, but as God would have it, Sonny was hired for a new job just a few miles away. Living out here became a unexpected priority for them. It was working out perfectly for all of us; Cindy and Sonny were helping us with our mortgage payments and we were about to be blessed by having our new grandson live with us.*

*Cindy and her baby came home the following night and "Pop Pop" had a chance to hold his new grandson for the first time. Cindy immediately requested that Bob not smoke on the lower level of the house, advising him that the smoke was not healthy for the baby. He agreed with Cindy's request but seemed resentful to be asked to monitor his behavior in his own house. Cindy's admonition must have made him feel uncomfortable, because a week later, he would tell me the details of a prayer he had made the very evening that the baby came home. It proved to be a very significant petition.*

"Lord," he began, "I know that my family has told me to stop smoking because they are concerned about my health. I know that I have ignored the doctor's orders to stop after my triple bypass. Gloria says that I am sinning against You by continuing to offend the Holy Spirit. But Lord, You know how much I love to smoke. I never thought You would want to take this pleasure away from me. I know that I am stubborn. I guess, if You really want me to stop You'll have to give me another heart attack."

*Little Vincent was asleep with his parents when I intruded into their apartment early Saturday morning with the news that an ambulance was on its way to take*

Bob to the hospital. He had awoken to a heart attack a short time before, on the morning after his prayer.

I was in high gear, as always in an emergency, insisting that a dose of T.P.A. be administered as soon as we got to the trauma center of the local hospital that was just blocks away. It is hard to get bureaucracy moving when the protocol is testing before treatment, despite the fact that there was no question that Bob was in the middle of a major attack. I kept pushing the doctors along to administer the shot and I feel that I was somewhat successful in avoiding severe heart damage by my prodding. My interference may not have been appreciated by the staff, but I was encouraged to act by our previous experience with the progress of heart muscle damage.

Bob waited a week to tell me about his prayer. It is amazing to me that he did not immediately connect his heart attack with an answer from the Lord. I imagine he was too busy joking with the hospital staff to even notice that he had just been pushed off his feet by the command of the Almighty as a faithful answer to his prayer. Bob was right, the Lord does have a good sense of humor. Bob had once again gotten what he had asked for, a direct answer from God and he has not smoked another cigarette since.

In spite of early intervention, he did suffer additional damage according to his tests. Yet he is even more vigorous now than he was when he was younger. He is a walking miracle. He has never felt depressed or incapacitated in spite of his heart trouble and he credits the Lord with giving him the knowledge that he would be all right during the critical first hours of his last attack.

*The doctor that has followed his case since his first hospitalization cannot believe that he is feeling as well as he looks.*

*A recent diagnosis of diabetes has not daunted Bob one bit either. He takes his medicine, watches his food intake more carefully, but most of all, he has complete faith in the Lord to keep him where He wants him to be. We learned from Regina's death firsthand that death is not a bad event to a believer. It is only the act of passing on to a place that we are destined to go for eternity, a place that Jesus has prepared for us in advance.*

"Let not your heart be troubled; believe in God, believe also in Me. In my Father's house there are many dwelling places; if it were not so, I would have told you; for I go to prepare a place for you. And if I go and prepare a place for you, I will come again, and receive you to myself; that where I am, there you may be also."( John 14:1,2,3)

"Truly, truly I say to you, he who hears My word and believes Him who sent Me, has eternal life, and does not come into judgment, but has passed out of death into life."( John 5:24.)

*Bob and I both feel no fear of leaving this earth. We hope to be here to see our new crop of babies grow for many years, but we are not daunted at the thought that we may be called for sooner.*

*For the rest of our lives we plan to be attuned to listening for God's voice to direct our paths. We share our insights freely with one another and other seekers of the Lord. We depend on the Holy Spirit to guide our decisions. We have both lost our innate impulsiveness* and gained a patient awareness that is open to the guidance of the Holy Spirit to direct us in our choices. Most of all, our days are filled with a sense of wonder at His works.

The Holy Spirit is so personal. He is both God and part of us at the same time. God the Father gave us a means to understand this mystery by presenting Himself in Jesus as man and God at the same time. Because the Spirit of God is indwelling, He understands what it takes to communicate personally to each of us in terms we intimately understand. He speaks every language on earth and can minister to every believer at the same time. Living in the computer age has made this concept much easier for people to understand. If man's limited mind can invent a system that can communicate with multitudes of people at once, just imagine what the Inventor of man is capable of. We cannot even begin to fathom the possibilities of how God's mind works.

The Holy Spirit also protects us. He is wise to every evil trick of Satan. He can warn us of danger, give us solutions to problems and let us know when we are reacting against the will of God. He can convey our prayers to Jesus and deliver the answers through dreams, ideas, an inner persuasive voice or even in the person of angels to direct us. He is our teacher, our helper, our comforter and our most intimate friend. Jesus himself promised to send Him to us.

> "But I tell you the truth, it is to your advantage that I go away; for if I do not go away, the Helper shall not come to you; but if I go, I will send Him to you." (John 16:7)

"But when He, the Spirit of truth, comes, He will guide you into all the truth; for He will not speak on His own initiative, but whatever He hears, He will speak; and He will disclose to you what is to come. He shall glorify Me; for He shall take of Mine, and shall disclose it to you. All things that the Father has are Mine; therefore I said, that He takes of Mine, and will disclose it to you."
(John 16:13,14,15)

*We have instant access to Him when we open our eyes hearts and ears to hear His message. If we deliberately sin, (yes, in spite of good intentions Christians do), He retreats from our conscious mind. He is part of the Godhead and cannot reside in a place of sin. That is why our bodies are to be regarded as God's temple. If we invite Him in, He will come immediately. It is important to remember He is a Gentleman and will not go where He is not wanted.*

*He is the performer of miracles, instant healings, and can give us superhuman strength both physical and emotional. He is the one who told Bob that my words saying Regina was "healed" were the words that were sent by God to answer Bob's direct petition for her "healing". Bob had never used those words except in his private journal entries, yet the Spirit directed me to use them when I spoke to Bob, and the Spirit told Bob they were from God. God did send His Comforter to Bob, caring in a loving personal way for his grief stricken servant, and He still managed to run the universe at the same time. There is so much mystery to look forward to solving when we each get to Heaven.*

*Dying is not a bad thing. We commonly use the word dying to mean the end of life, but it really does not apply to a believer. Biblically, death is strictly a term reserved for the unredeemed. Death, in the Bible, is referred to as the "wages of sin." It is the dreadful reward for a sinful life. It implies total separation from God. The Biblical term for the passing-on of believers is "sleep." The Scripture implies that believers have no awareness of separation, but pass peacefully on to eternity.*

*What does the believer have to look forward to? In this life, we have the comfort of prayer to God and communion with the Holy Spirit. With faith, the gift we receive for our surrender to God's will, we have the ability to overcome worldly discomforts and also have the peaceful knowledge that a better existence is promised to us forevermore. The pity is that the promise is there for all humanity, just for the asking, and so many of us fail to ask.*

*A skeptic, my husband, weakened by the plight of his child, took a bold step and asked the Lord to prove Himself. The greatest strengthening of faith that Bob had, was the physical death of the child that he had prayed for. Through her passing on and the signs and wonders that God performed for us, both our faiths became unshakable. We no longer question God's reality in our daily lives even in the smallest degree. How can we, when He has given us so much tangible evidence of His existence and the resurrection of His children?*

*What were we left with when Bob's daughter passed on? The answer is peace and joy. By having faith we saw His miracles and by seeing His miracles we received peace and comfort. Prolonged grief flees from the heart*

221

*of someone who absolutely knows their loved one is in Heaven. Sorrow over separation, sentimental tears over memories and feelings of loneliness are always left, but are countered by the hopes of our future reunion in Heaven.*

*My preoccupation with our children, plus our busy show schedule, kept me from fulfilling Bob's wishes for a speedily written account of his diary. I had written intermittently for four years without any sense of urgency about the book's completion. Early in 1998, I suddenly began to feel an inner urge to complete the task I had started in 1993. One day, I sat at the computer, feeling a strong drive to finish the last chapters of this book. Bob walked into the room and asked what I was writing. I responded that I was about to seriously tackle the completion of the book and was preparing to send some inquiries to publishers.*

*Bob shook his head incredulously and with a sly smile went into our bedroom and came back with a sheet of paper. The paper held the names of several professional ghost writers whom he was about to contact for the purpose of completing the job I had started years ago.*

*Bob then explained he'd been feeling that I had no intention of going on with the book, and rather than force me to continue with a project that I seemed disinterested in, he had decided to give his notes to someone else in order to fulfill the promise he had made to the Lord. An account of his diary had to be written as a public testimony of his faith. He would not go back on his promise to God even if he had to circumvent me as his partner in the task. When I resumed my writing, it* was only two days away from Bob's deadline for my resumption of work on the book. He was ready to contact another writer.

We were again a part of another miracle of the Holy Spirit. The Spirit had convicted me with guilt over my lapse in dedication to our project and had given me an overwhelming desire to get back to work. Bob had, after prayer, set a date after which I would be excluded from writing his account. My resumption of writing was in perfect timing with his desire to get the book finished. God, through the working of the Holy Spirit, reunified our efforts to glorify His name and left us once again feeling humbled by His faithfulness and His perfect sense of timing.

Instead of being disappointed at my tardiness to achieve our goal, my husband was aglow with gratitude to God. Instead of my hurt and guilt at disappointing my husband, I was left with a strengthening of my mission to serve him as a faithful wife. God had turned an awkward moment in our marriage into a victory of love, both to each other and to Him. May He continue to do so, as long as we both shall live and hopefully even beyond this earthbound existence. And more importantly, may our experiences with the Almighty inspire others to seek Him and receive the bountiful gift of faith and assurance that he has so generously and patiently bestowed on us.

God's answers came to our family through revelations, inner voices, physical changes, and angelic interventions. We encourage others to seek God in prayer and wait for His answers, which most certainly will become apparent in time. Prayer undoubtedly is *connected to personal miracles for the faithful seeker of His response. Persevere in faith and you will not miss the connection.*

# Chapter 17
## Epilogue–A Closing Note on Prayer

People tend to think that good or bad luck can change lives and that their future can be influenced by chance. There is only one way to know, without doubt, that it is God who is intervening in our lives and answering our needs. We must first make those needs known to God through prayer.

Consider the mystery of prayer. Surely God sees us and knows our hearts already. How can we empower God to act when He already possesses all infinite power? He knows our needs and personal misfortunes already. He can reverse all that plagues us at His will. And He does do that according to His will, but without our petitioned prayer how will we know for sure that it is He who answers us?

God has designed prayer as a perfect vehicle to connect the relationship between our need and His will. He graciously extends the offer of an amazing, supernatural, one on one relationship with each believer. By choosing to pray, we open an intimate communication line with

God through which we receive obvious direction in the management of our daily lives.

Prayer ensures the growth of faith. It gives us stamina and endurance when we grapple with life's inevitable problems. Best of all, God's response to our prayers gives us an extraordinary sense of inner peace. It assures us that He is ever present in our lives through the presence of His Holy Spirit and His works.

Prayer establishes the connection.

## AN INVITATION TO THE READER

The Mascarelli's have plans for a sequel to *The Prayer Connection*. Their forthcoming book *The Miracle Connection* will focus on the stories of other individuals or families who have experienced an extraordinary event as a miraculous answer to prayer.

The authors welcome contributions from their readers. They must be typed, double spaced on 8½"x11" numbered pages. The writer's name must appear on each page at the heading. Please include your name address and phone number on the first page. A telephone interview will be arranged If your story is considered for publication. Please allow 90 days for a reply. Send correspondence to the address listed below. Please include a stamped, self addressed envelope if you wish to have your article returned.

Contributions to *The Miracle Connection* will be carefully read for suitability to the project. Submitted stories must refer to first person experiences. The authors seek true stories that revolve around an event or events which are verifiable.

If you have any comments on *The Prayer Connection* that you would like to share with the authors, you may write to Gloria Mascarelli care of:

Miracle Book Publishers
P.O.Box 429
Patchogue, NY 11772

Gloria and Bob Mascarelli are nationally recognized authors and authorities on Oriental antiques. They have authored *Warman's Oriental Antiques* and co-authored *Wallace-Homestead Price Guide to Oriental Antiques.* Currently they participate in numerous antique shows throughout the country. They live in the suburbs of Long Island, New York. This is their first book about personal experiences.

"Writing *The Prayer Connection,* was a soul searching experience for me," reports Gloria. "I found it difficult to present myself in an unfavorable light, yet the truthful nature of the book forced me to be candidly honest in my presentation of the background material that enhanced Bob's journal. I did not always like the person that I was. I often found her selfish and self-serving . Yet, I had to present myself as I was at the time. Also, I had some reluctance to write about Regina's suicide. Writing about my episodes of guilt often brought back feelings of remorse that left me saddened for many days. But, along with these sorrows, came immense joy. Revealing Bob's growth as a Christian and the miracles that we both encountered was a blessed experience."

Bob, with his characteristic humor reports that Gloria is a far better writer than she is a housekeeper. "Since she has the talent for words that I lack, I took over the household responsibilities while she worked on the book. I learned that I am a very good cook, a God given talent that I never would have discovered if this book wasn't written." In a more serious tone, Bob reports, "I promised God that this book would be written before I was even sure that He existed. It was part of a bartering deal I made with Him. If He would answer my prayers, I would glorify His name. It doesn't seem like a very respectful way to approach God now that I am a believer, but it seemed appropriate at that time. Amazingly, God took me at my word and gave me proof upon proof that He was responding to my Prayers. He took me from the depths of despair to the heights of revelation and I will praise Him here on earth until the day I can praise Him as part of His heavenly kingdom."

# Order form

Phone orders: 1 (800) 478-7188
Fax orders: (516) 207-3175

*The Prayer Connection*

| No. of copies | Cost | Total |
|---|---|---|
| ——— | @ $14.95 | ——— |
| Shipping and handling | $ 3.95 | ——— |
| (please add $0.95 for | | |
| each additional copy.) | Subtotal | ——— |
| | | |
| (NYS residents only) | Tax | ——— |
| Sales tax of 8 ¼% | | |
| | Total | ——— |

I am enclosing a check for $ ———
(payable to: Miracle Book Publishers)

Charge card information:
☐Visa    ☐Mastercard

Account No... ————————————————
Exp. date ————

Print Name ————————————————
Signature ————————————————
Address ————————————————
————————————————

Telephone (    ) ————————————
Mail to:

Miracle Book Publishers
PO Box 429
Patchogue, NY 11772

For speaking engagements please contact the authors at (516) 207-3174.
For Volume orders or non-profit organization discounts please contact the
publisher at the address or phone number listed above.